BEYOND

FACE VALUE

The Story of Romel Ravello

ROMEL RAVELLO

First Published in 2014

This edition published in USA, 2016

Copyright © 2014 by Romel Ravello

All rights reserved

This book or any portion thereof may not be reproduced or used in any manner whatsoever without the express written permission of the publisher

except for the use of brief quotations in a book review.

Xulon Press

USA

Dedication/Acknowledgment

Glory and honor, and blessings and power be unto the Lord God, who has preserved my life to this point that my story could be told, displaying His awesome power and might. I dedicate this work to Him; the One who has
begun and continue to do His marvelous work in my life. Also, to my mother Denyse Ravello-Gift who passed on to be with the Lord February, 2016. I thank the Lord for her love and commitment in bringing us up to the best of her ability. To my siblings Ricardo, Randy, and Rachel I am eternally grateful, for having allowed me
to share some of our most personal childhood stories with the world. I need to thank also Mr. Scott Rimer for being such a blessing to my life and writing the introduction for this book and Ms. Kimlee Bunraj for editing my many mistakes.

God is good all the time, and all the time God is good; it's been a painful experience losing my mom but in accordance to His wonderful grace and love God I press on towards my Mission 10,000 thanking God for her life; The greatest blessing I've ever received. This one goes out to all of you!

Foreword

Here I sit trying to find the correct words to describe my friend. Did God send me a message about life that I was not seeing? Or was it pure coincidence that I was asking God to show me a beacon of hope for humanity mere seconds before meeting him. In the end it will not matter. For I have met a new friend and a new brother. Though we have only known each other for a short period, I feel as If I have known him since the beginning of time. In Romel you find the embodiment of what God put us on this earth to achieve.

I struggled to find a way to describe my friend. I felt my best effort could not come from my limited experience of life compared to the rollercoaster life of Romel Ravello. Many times when I read a book I find the words to be empty and meaningless. Without thought provoking substance. In an effort to avoid this I chose to go back to a period of time when words were carefully chosen. Men were very purposeful in what they spoke as it was a matter of character. In many ways I believe technology has helped us loose this quality in communication. Social media has created chaos that is hard to follow with the instant speed and lack of context. In my attempt to introduce Romel as a learned man to the world, I have chosen a book published in 1923, by Arthur Brisbane: "The Book of Today".

It is in this book that I found a way to best describe my friend, my brother and his effort to make our world a better place to live, to love, to fall and get up, and most of all to see the beauty of a world that shines through his eyes like a beacon of hope.

"The little child in the doorway on the poor street looks in wonder at the face of the old man, furrowed, sad and discouraged.

The old man, whose questioning and striving with fate has been answered by failure, looks down upon the little child, and in that child's face and hopefulness and helplessness finds a partial answer at least to the great question.

He knows that his own life need not be a failure in reality, although it has failed on the surface.

He knows to protect one such child, to give it an hour's happiness or save it from a day of suffering is alone worthwhile.

His clothes are Torn, his shoes are worn, his face is sad with the disappointments and mistakes of many years.

He looks at the child, whose face is a page with no line written upon it, whose eyes reflect the wonders and all the beauty of truth and innocence, and looking at the child he is able to answer the question, saying to himself:

I am here to help others, to use the power wisely if it comes, and to endure poverty bravely if it must come. I am here to not think of myself but of others, to think of children such as this and to help them and protect them."

It is in my mind's eyes that my friend was able to see both paths of the lives described. The ability to rise above the adversity that was thrust upon our author, is truly found in his belief in a Higher Power, his Lord, his Redeemer, Christ Jesus. One that he felt had abandoned him, until that fateful day that the spirit of God, revealed His plan for my brother's life work.

There are not many who are chosen to fulfill this calling, but he is. There are not many who would accept it with unbridled enthusiasm and steadfast determination, but he has! I have been lucky and truly blessed to meet one of the true believers in the higher power and the greater ability that is the Blood of the Lamb. And oh, what a gift it is to just spend ten minutes looking into those eyes with ancient wisdom. May God bless every step of Romel's journey! For it is being done out of pure love for his fellow man to the glory of God our Father, His Holy Spirit, and to the glory of our Lord and Savior Jesus Christ.

Scott A. Rimer

Preface:

The Story of Romel Ravello

I am going to do something ridiculously crazy for God, something that no one else is trying to do, or even thinking of doing. Something unique and dynamic. I want to be like a Moses or an Abraham, a David, or a Jeremiah, an Elijah or an Elisha. I want to be a man that will stand up and proclaim the goodness of God's loving mercy and grace, like Paul! Yeah I want to be like Paul, to forsake everything so that I might press forward towards the mark of the higher calling that is in Christ Jesus, just like Paul.

Chapter I

Humble Beginnings

My name is Romel Ravello and I was born in the Caribbean island, Trinidad, of the Twin Island Republic Trinidad and Tobago on the day of December 19th 1988. My mother Denyse Ravello already had three other children, Ricardo, Randy and Rachel, and was living in abject poverty. My father skipped out from the time of my conception, declaring immediately that I, whoever I may turn out to be, was certainly not his child!

My earliest recollection of my life is sleeping on a bench around the Queen's Park Savannah with my mom, my two brothers and my sister. I was about four years old. This scene would set the tone of my childhood to the end of my teenage years. We spent almost an entire week sleeping around that park. I can only imagine what might have happened had it been the rainy season. My mother was originally from the Northeastern town of Morvant, but I have never, to this day, asked how we ended up homeless and sleeping around the Queen's Park Savannah that week when the rest of our family, including my grandmother and several aunts, all had houses to live in.

Another thing I never found out was exactly where we lived before my first memory. Those questions, like many others along my walk of life, still remain unanswered. Finally after what seemed to be an eternity of discomforting days and restlessness, starless nights came to an end when we moved into an apartment in another Northeastern town called San Juan. The apartment comprised of two 15' x 15' rooms, an outhouse in the backyard and a stand pipe just outside the front door. There was no electricity; no water inside and barely had a roof. The apartment was not fit enough for even a dog to live in, but to us it was home and we were ever grateful to finally have one.

The first couple of years were very hard on my family. My mother was not employed and all of my siblings were under the age of ten, with none of us being in a position to help ourselves improve our living conditions. There were many days that we had to go without food, surviving mainly on green mangoes from the tree out in the front yard or other fruits around. Sometimes we had no mangoes and would be forced to go many days on as much water as our tiny stomachs could possibly hold, but at least we had water! It was only after growing older that I came to realize many families which may have had access to food and proper shelter, still had no access to pipe-borne water for many, many miles.

Occasionally, various neighbors would give us some food to eat if we were lucky. I can remember countless times when we would receive just one plate of food and my mother, being as loving and caring as she knew how, would divide the plate of food into four portions for us kids and she herself would remain hungry. There were other times when we would even pick and cook some of the wild bushes growing along the side of the apartment.

Our living conditions slowly improved as we started attending the Febeau Open Bible Church, one of the local churches on Laventille Road, San Juan. One whose pastor was contented with being as good of a sheppard to the little flock that God had entrusted him with, rather than going about seeking new sheep to add to his fold. Maybe this was the reason why Pastor Michael McKenna was so loved and respected above all the ministers within the community. No matter the reason, everyone loved him and it was quite rare in a small island like Trinidad, to find ministers of the Lord who had their reputations perfectly intact.

As we began to fellowship more and more within the church, my hunger and passion to serve God rapidly increased. This was mainly due to the fact that, growing up without a single toy to play with, fellowship with the church and my new found friends was just about the most amount of fun I was going to get out of life and I enjoyed it to the fullest. I first started off by joining the junior choir and then later joined the kids Sunday School where I often specialized in playing the part of some Old Testament prophet or the other. But my passion was not to offer beautiful songs of praise onto the Lord as a choirboy, nor was it me acting illustrations of the life for the prophets of old.

One day our Sunday School was going to another church in the capital city of Port of Spain to visit their Sunday School class to conduct a session between both these classes. Apparently that class came over to our Sunday School before I started and everyone but me and my siblings, was aware that there would need to be a young Preacher to deliver a powerful sermon. This sermon needed to be able to capture and captivate the attention of almost fifty peers, ranging from toddlers to pre-teen boys and girls. The sermon would also have to be preached in such a way that all the children at the end would be able to actively participate in a Q&A about the sermon for about an hour.

As soon as our teacher explained this to the class my mind instantly went to work. I could see myself in the best clothes I owned, preaching a sermon which I had been practicing in front of the tiny face mirror at home. It was to be a story from the book of Romans depicting how the devil comes as a thief in the night to kill, steal and destroy. At this time Rachel, Randy and Ricardo, my siblings, turned and smiled a silly little childish grim at me, all at the exact same time. To the members of my family it was already evident that God had set me aside for a purpose and plan He had ordained, even from the time of my conception in the womb. As expected I was selected to preach and boy did I preach. I preached my heart out to those little kids, my peers. But it was not a sermon that only had the full attention of the Sunday School class. I caused even the pastor of the adult church service to stop in his tracks and had the entire church congregation listening in pin-drop silence!

This was evidence to me that God had called me to do His work. It was simple to me. All I was doing was having fun in my own way just like any other child my age. However, the strange events of the following Monday night forced me to think differently for a short while.

Chapter II

On Fire

There was a Three Night Crusade carded for that week at the Febeau Open Bible Church, our home church starting on a Monday night with a battery of powerful and dynamic mighty men and women of God from all over the island coming to preach and teacher the word of God. It was opening night and our small church was filled beyond capacity. Not even on New Year's Eve had I seen the pews filled with so many people. The service started around 6:00pm and ended at 9:30pm. Sometime shortly after 9:00pm there was a pastor preaching about what I have not the slightest clue as I was (together with about 95% of the children my age) fast asleep. However, it must have had something to do with children because I found myself being awaken to the unpleasant instruction to walk to the front of the altar along with every other child present in the church, to be anointed with oil and prayed for.

I can't remember what my initial feelings toward the instruction was but I was no more than six years old and knowing myself, I could say my feeling most likely would have been that of vexation and contempt. I stood up in front the altar, somewhere along the seemingly endless line of children, next to my sister and brothers. The only thing I could remember about this pastor coming down the line, taking his time to earnestly pray for each individual child then sending them back to their parents, was that he was wearing these really large shoes! Like a clown, Ronald McDonald the clown! This I remember thinking to myself, as I fought off the desire to return to the soft, warm nest of my mother's lap without being prayed for. Had it not been for my sister, who certainly would have told on me, I would have attempted to rush right back. So I stood there, waiting, waiting to be prayed for, but only so that I could go back to sleep. Finally, he was praying for Caleb standing next to me, which meant I was next in line and soon to be in dreamland.

As the pastor in the red shoes stood in front of me, he called for the oil which he placed in the palm of his hand and took a step towards me, closed his eyes and began to stretch out his hand to place it on my forehead. As his hand was about to gently connect with my forehead so that he might begin to pray for me, he suddenly withdrew his hand, opened his eyes and stared at me. A long, hard, deep and intense stare, which at first puzzled me but as he continued to stare I began to feel afraid. My fears was evident to him and he smiled at me and simply said "fear not my child, stand right there."

Stand right there! Now I was beyond worried, I did not know what to think of it. Did he see some sort of bad thing I did and was about to school me in front of such a large crowd? Was something bad about to happen in my life which God revealed it to this man in the big red shoes?

I have heard many stories of prophets, both in the Bible and in the present times, of how God revealed secrets about past, present and future events to them and reasoned with myself that this was happening.

My mind raced as to why he changed the course he was on and paused before he prayed for me. I was now fully awake and that was a good thing as he un-expectedly to everyone present, skipped me and moved on to pray for Rachel, then Randy, then my oldest brother Ricardo and all the other kids that were also waiting in line after us, until I was the only person before the alter to be prayed for. Again the visiting pastor stood in front of me and stared me in the eye. This went on without him speaking a single word and me shaking in my boots for about an eternal five minutes. Finally he called for a microphone to be brought forward, which he took and turned to the congregation to ask whose son I was. When my mother stood to her feet, the red shoed pastor asked that she bring my entire family to the altar so that I may receive a word from God. My mother, my sister and two brothers came up front and for the second time in two days, I found myself surrounded by pin-drop silence as everyone listened to what God was declaring over my life. "A multitude of people, a sea of human lives, hearts and faith touched, standing behind the altar preaching the word of God." This was the word of God he proclaimed over my life.

Chapter III

Let the Water Flow!

There was something special that would happen whenever I would pray. It was as if I had a direct line to the throne room of God. A great example would be the first time in my life I had eaten pizza. I could not have been older than six years old and my mother had just received her first Social Welfare cheque. She had promised us that when she did receive it, she would take us out for pizza and the day had finally come. The cheque came in the mail at the post office and my eldest brother Ricardo raced home waving it in the air with much excitement and delight. All we had to do was each take a shower, get dressed and be on our way to what seemed to me to be a better standard of living.

There was a very good reason why God selected that particular piece of Scripture in Romans for me to deliver three weeks earlier. Because, like a thief in the night, the devil came in and attempted to steal my joy, kill my hopes and destroy my moment of happiness to come. Out of all the days of the year, there was no water in the tap on this day! My mother decided that since there was no water in the pipe, she would go purchase the pizza and bring it back home for us, but my mind was set more on the kids play park in the car parking lot of the pizzeria than on the pizza itself. My young heart immediately felt crush as I walked outside to turn the tap and see for myself that there was in fact no water.

Tears flowed freely down my cheek as I slowly accepted that I was not going to the play park today. My mother was already dressing and at the same time instructing my eldest brother to ensure that no one was to leave the apartment until she returns. Suddenly it came to me! God gave me that sermon to preach so that I would understand and believe that there was power in the name of Jesus. That even though the devil may come to steal, kill and destroy, Jesus came and gave us the gift of eternal life and that He gives all good things to those who loves Him and those who would simply have faith that He is able. I had already accepted Him as my personal Lord and Savior and all I needed to do was to ask in His name and I would receive.

Pizza, I weighed in the balance was a good thing and therefore God wanted me to have it. So I held on to that pipe, closed my eyes and pretended to pray in the way that a pastor would when he was praying for a miracle. I opened my mouth and in a commending voice said "Heavenly Father in the mighty name of Jesus Christ, I rebuke every attack of the devil towards my happiness and I command in the name of Jesus that water will flow from this pipe". Instantaneously, before I could even finish speaking it into being, it happened! The water gushed out of the tap like it had never gushed before. What's more, from that day on, there was never again a time that there was no water in that pipe.

Another noteworthy time of powerful prayer and faith that only a small child could have, was the week of the storm. I think 1995 was the year. There was a hurricane passing through Trinidad and the entire island was under storm watch. Everyone was advised to remain indoors and stay away from doors and windows. The rain was pouring and the wind was raging to the extent that many roofs had blown off houses and buildings. One such building which had their roof blown off was our local church. Inside of my family's two room apartment, we had one mattress on the floor that the five of us would sleep on. There were so many holes in our roof that the mattress was totally soaking wet. But maybe then, the many holes in the roof may have been the same key factor that caused our roof not to blow off. God works in mysterious ways, doesn't He!

The hardest part about the storm was that we had absolutely no food at all in the house. It was day three of the State of Emergency storm watch and I was dying of hunger, although it was always the norm for us to not have food at home. Surviving most days from one of the neighbors providing us with a plate of food, but in the middle of the storm, there was no neighbour that we would have gone to.

I was left without a choice but to once again cry out to God to deliver me from my distress. It was also to my advantage that our pastor had recently preached a sermon on David crying out to God to save him out of all his troubles once again. So I prayed, I prayed like David and cried out to God in a loud voice. My siblings looked at me as if I were going crazy, but I could still remember the glance of hope in my sister's eyes. Hope that God would hear my cry, as He so often in the past.

My sister, somehow, always knew exactly when God was working in my life. She would often tell me that sometimes she would look at me and see me glowing and that's how she knew that God is at work. But during that storm, God did not reveal even to her what He was about to do. I prayed and cried out to God for about three minutes then stopped. Suddenly I realized that I did not know how exactly God was going to save me from my troubles as they were so far different from the mighty army that David had come up against in the sermon a few Sundays ago. I searched my tiny brain for a way to ask God to deliver me from my distress, then I remembered a play that my Sunday School class had done some time back and I knew then what I had to ask God to do for me.

"Lord Father in the name of Jesus open up the heavens and let Manna fall out of the sky as you did with the children of Israel when they were in the wilderness, so that we your children would be hungry no more."

I called out to God and in childlike faith, hope and expectation, I expected Him to show up and answer my prayer as He has done many times gone by. But if Manna was going to fall from the sky I thought to myself, then I would have to go outside to collect it so that we could eat it. I raced to the door with a big smile expecting to see food raining from the heavens like the days of old. You see, I had come to the blind undoubting frame of mind that my God was the same yesterday, today and forevermore. He did it back then and He would certainly do it again and save me, His child that He loves unconditionally.

I grabbed hold of one of the dining room chairs, dragged it to the door and climbed up on it to unlock the door. I would usually struggle to unlatch the top lock on the door, but this time I was strong in spirit so I unlatched it with such ease that my mother had not yet noticed what I was up to. I moved the chair and unlatched the bottom latch. Pushing forward in faith, I flung the door wide open. Immediately the powerful wind of the hurricane slammed it back in my face. The force was so great that a plate fell off a shelf and broke. This alerted my family that I was up to something, but I got so caught up in the Spirit that as the wind blew the door back in, I, with the very same speed as the wind, rebuked every attack of the devil and pushed the door open once again, this time with a supernatural authority that can only come from knowing that God has your back in a particular situation.

I ran out into the pouring rain and lifted my hands to the heavens and cried out to the Lord, God. My mother ran out in a mad rage after me, grabbed on to my soaking wet body and started to pull me inside, In return I cried out to be left alone and wrestled with her informing her that God was about to send Manna from heaven. I could never forget the look she gave me at that moment. A look that said she thought I might have some serious mental problems. However, before the moment in which she gave me that look was over, Manna fell from the sky!

My mother looked at me once more, this time with a shameful look as I could differentiate between the rain and the tears that gently started rolling down her cheeks. All she could say was "I'm sorry, I will never again doubt when you tell me God is going to do something." For you see, the hurricane was so fierce that the wind blew the roof off our local church and someone living next door to the church phoned the pastor to inform him of what was happening. In the middle of the storm, Pastor Michael McKenna left the comfort and safety of his house to go the church building in order to secure what needed to be protected from the rains.

While he was in his office, he came across a box of supermarket goods and various snacks, of which he later testified that he had no idea where it came from. After securing what he could, he was moved by the Spirit to take the box of food along with him on his way home. At the exact moment that I had figured out that it was Manna that I wanted God to make fall from the sky, God's Spirit placed it into my pastor's heart that he was to drop the food stuff and snacks off at our house, which was less than five minutes away from the church compound.

As my mother angrily held on to my soaking body, squeezing me tightly so that I would calm down and return my crazy self to the house with her, she suddenly stopped and released me, looking off to her left in utter disbelief. As I also turned and looked up the hill that was leading down towards our house, there was Pastor Mc Kenna coming down the hill with a very big box in his hand. A box full of deliverance, all to the power and glory and honor of the Lord Jesus Christ. He says in Matthew 19:14,

> *"Let the little children come to me, and stop keeping them away, because the kingdom belongs to people like these."*

In my present state of life, I am longing to once again possess that kind of faith in God that I had as a small child. I would move mountains and walk across the sea according to the will of God if I had now, half the unshakeable faith I had back then. Word spread like wildfire about God delivering me and my family by answering my prayer for Manna to fall from the sky. By the time pastor was finished with his testimony the following Sunday, under the sun at church (the church after all had no roof) he had also spoken of how God had displayed how great and powerful He was. Pastor unveiled to us that very day a blueprint to a marvelous facility that God had laid out before him to replace our small wooden church. It would have been a difficult endeavor for our pastor to have done on his own and therefore God stepped in and did it for him. From the time the roof was gone, we all already knew that it was time to start something new. Pastor then called me up to the altar, anointed my head with oil and prayed for me. All of my peers decided it would be funny to nickname me "Pastor Garvin". A name that did not sit well with me at all.

Chapter IV

Peer Pressure

With all the gifts the spirit of God had endowed me with from my youth, He probably withheld the gift of spiritual wisdom for a greater purpose that He had intended from the start. The nickname Pastor Garvin caused everyone my age to laugh and I was very upset over the whole thing. It was only much later on in life that I was able to see that it was actually another direct assault against my life by the devil who was constantly going around trying to devour me and destroy God's plan over my life. I could honestly say that I allowed him to get to me. I got so angry that I stopped praying altogether, stopped attending Sunday School and lost all delight in listening to the word of God. I never made myself available for acting in any other future plays after that issue.

The devil was happy. He felt like he was a success after a short while as God was totally out of my mind. I occupied my time by playing ordinary children games and doing the things my other peers were doing. I roamed the neighborhood for fruit trees to climb and went swimming in the nearby river. It took some time, but I finally went back to being just Garvin instead of Pastor Garvin. It felt good not to be the laughing stock of the community.

In any other part of the world, it may have been a nice nickname but not in Trinidad. In spite of the devil feeling as though he had victory over my life, God always had His plan and I understand now that the devil actually played right into God's hand by making me act in such the brutal way that he did. God always has a plan! Because I stopped spending most of my free time at church, the envelop of poverty quickly reminded me of how depressing my life circumstances were. Worst yet, I knew of a better living condition but it came along with that nickname that I ever so hated at that point in time. Instead, I continued to rebel against the word of God. The first of many rebellions throughout my life.

I really never liked Christmas. It was the time of year when it was most evident as to exactly how poor my family really was. We never had a special Christmas, never had a lot of food, or decorations, nor did we received any gifts except for one special year thanks to one special guy and his family. It was the year 1994 and I was six years old. Nigel, a gentleman that lived across the river from us, most likely was talking to his dad who had been giving us food stuff the entire month of December and I think he probably realized that without his intervention my siblings and I would not have had Christmas for yet another year. I personally thought nothing of it, but I can still remember the look of hopelessness on the face of my sister my brother Randy. Randy even came over to me and apologized about the whole Pastor Garvin ordeal, claiming responsibility for start the entire taunt. It was as if he was trying to find some sort of a way to ask me to pray to God for us to have a good Christmas that year. However, I still refused to even entertain the idea of praying again.

I was too scared that God would in fact answer my prayer and the teasing would repeat itself once more. I am thankful that my Father in heaven knows what I need before I can even ask Him for it (Matthew 6:8). He says in His word that though we might turn away from Him, his hands are always stretched out towards us and even though I refused to pray, God decided that He was going to receive glory this day yet!

It was about 3:30pm on December 24th when I heard Nigel calling out to me from across the river. I was almost sure he was calling me for a plate of food as the neighbors would usually call me if they had something to give to our family. I was always favored over my two brothers and my sister. As I made my way across the river, I was sadden to see Nigel with both hands swinging. He had to have been calling me for something else, I thought, hoping that something was not some type of work for I was far too weak from being hungry.

As I entered Nigel's living room, he instructed me to close my eyes as he removed a sheet that covered something on the table. Then he called for me to open them and as I did so, my eyes instantly lit up and my hunger immediately vanished. There, on his table, were three of the most beautiful remote control cars I have ever seen, even to this present day. There was one yellow car, two red ones one Barbie Doll. He picked up the yellow one and wished me a Merry Christmas as he handed it over to me. The rest of toys he gave to me to carry for my siblings. It was the best Christmas ever! Santa Claus had finally visited my family was the idea I planted in my own mind. I was haunted however by the thought that God, somehow knowing my desires, had some part to play in all of this. Well at least I didn't have to pray and be teased for it I thought.

Chapter V

A World of Distractions

The gift of dynamic public speaking was instilled in me, but the devil, continuing his investment of destroying God's plan for my life, would keep me busy with so many different things. Things that I saw as wonderful and fulfilling. I did things that allowed me to gain the highest respect amongst the secular world and best of all no one was laughing! I was the biggest 'small thing' at the point in time.

My schooling had unofficially ended as I soon started to break classes with Randy. We would roam the entire island looking for yards to clean, cars to wash and people who we could generally beg for money. However, even though I was not attending school, my education in other useful skills increased rapidly. By the time I was eight years old, I learned the names of well over five hundred trees at the local botanical gardens and was conducting first class tours to the tourists that would arrive to our tropical paradise daily. By the age of ten I was without a doubt the best Tour Guide in the entire country. I was even offered a multimillion dollar contract by TIDCO "The Tourism Development Company" to do executive tours only on behalf of the Government of Trinidad and Tobago. Their one prerequisite was that I had to attend a six month course to receive my official Tour Guide License, which would have also put me in the Guinness Book of World Records as the youngest person in the world to be an official tour guide. My mouth watered at the idea of world fame, it immediately came to me that I really was the best tour guide in the country, maybe even in the world.

Cruise ships would arrive at the port in the capital city of Port of Spain and the tourists would get into buses in groups of twenty-five. These buses would then all have an official tour guide in them who would take the group on their island tour. They would visit one of our world famous beaches, Maracas Bay, Las Cuevas and other spots of interest across the island then it was back to the ship at around sunset. When these buses arrived at the Botanical Gardens in Port-of-Spain, (ironically the entrance to this garden sits directly across the street from the very same park bench my family and I lived on for almost a week years earlier) the tour guides in each bus would quickly tell their group about me and recommend that I be allowed to conduct the Botanical Gardens portion of the tour at no additional cost, but that they could feel free to tip me if liked. Most would agree and as they proceeded out of the buses, the tour guides would then merge together four different groups of tourists and lend me one of their loudspeakers. My twenty-five minute tour of the Botanical Gardens would consist of a group of one hundred persons, at the age of ten, when all other tour guides none younger than thirty toured groups of twenty-five.

Not only were my groups much larger than everyone else's, for the first few hours of each day, there was always a long line of buses with groups that decided that they were going to wait in line to have their garden tour conducted by Romel Ravello! Later on in the afternoon I would look for a group of 10-12 persons in the smaller buses and join them in the continuation of their tour from there to the very end. Some of the drivers of the smaller buses would even opt to not bring an official tour guide so that I would come along instead. It was economically better for the driver as he did not have to pay a tour guide also better for me in many ways, not just money wise and the tourists always had a better time with a kid who was better at his job and spoke far more clearly and understandably than any of the adult guides.

So, when I was approached by TIDCO, I happily accepted the offer. But like I said, I came to understand that it was part of Satan's plan to destroy my life because of the great things God had in store. I started the class and everything was going great. After the second week the teacher Ms. Kathryn Hackshaw even decided that I would also be a part-time teacher of the class. She would teach in the classroom and I would teach the class every time we went out on field trips, which was twice a week.

I was ever so delighted but so puffed up over the new position and power I received. I started looking down at the adults in my class and even within the entire tourism industry. I was unapproachable. If I had something to say to you, I would, and most times I had nothing good to say at all. However, for me, everything was going great. I was on my way to super stardom and that felt awesome. I am sure that you are aware that nothing that the devil has in store is ever good. He does not know the meaning of good. He rejected good when he rejected God. He wants only to destroy your life and to bring to naught the good things that your Father in heaven wants to bless you with and it seemed as if he was succeeding at this in my young life.

Just as he felt as though he had me in the palm of his hand, he pulled the carpet from below my feet. Carla Foderingham, one of the Directors of TIDCO at the time, also a news broadcaster for the 7pm news on the main television station channel in the country, called me into her office one day about a month into the class. She informed me that in order for me to continue the class and move on to sign a contract with the company, I would have to attend my ordinary school classes on a daily basis and at the end of each month I would need to summit a letter signed and stamped by the principle, stating how many days I attended school for the month.

I was not up to the task of attending school every day. It would have also been financially impossible for me to even attempt such a thing. Which right thinking ten year old, who happens to be the sole bread winner of his five member family, would give up making

US$150.00 per day to attend a school in which every teacher and student found him to be crazy? I was not! At school they found it too difficult to believe that a ten year old from the slums could have plans, visions, dreams and drive like I did. I had a plan to escape poverty and was establishing the contacts to do just that. The Prime Minister, his Cabinet, The Tourism Company TIDCO and a little leather bag filled with call cards of some of the most prestigious business men and women of the day, all who's attention I was granted exclusive access to at any time I needed or even wanted. Why would I give up on these things? I calmly asked her, as I took another gulp of my orange juice. She was unable to give me an answer. Maybe she was still in shock as a result of my hostility. "You can't do this to me!" I muttered under my breath, as my angry eyes made contact with her puzzled eyes.

The Prime Minister at the time, the Honourable Basdeo Panday, had earlier that morning given me two tickets for The 1999 Miss Universe Pageant being held in Trinidad and Tobago, later that week. There was a parade of the contestants through the streets of the capital city and for the entire time, I was captivated by the beauty and charm of Miss Peru and the girl at her left Miss Chile. I wanted Miss Peru to win so bad, there was just something about her that was special. I don't know what it was, but it was there.

The pageant took place at the Chaguaramas Hanger, an old, run down building that the U.S. Navy used back in World War II. It was never one of my favorite tour spots, but today, at the Miss Universe Pageant it was totally transformed. We found our seats and the show started shortly after. I thought that it was the most spectacular event ever displayed in my nation. I thank God for the opportunity. I had to get as close as I could to get some pictures of Miss Peru. I left my seat and headed stage side for some close up photos. I then proceeded to head back to my seat and turned around for one last photo. Suddenly, she was waving happily at me as Miss Chile spoke something into her ear. "Wow", I remember thinking, "they remembered me, awesome!" "Guess you're not backing Nicole Dyer?" (Our Trinidad and Tobago representative), someone chuckled to me, as I returned to my seat with a look of contentment, "Nicole who?" I replied with a big grin on my face. "Thanks for bringing me with you" my mother said as she rubbed my head in sweet delight.

I knew she still loved me dearly in spite of all the trouble I had given her in the past recent years. Besides, my trouble as a small child often came with good economics benefits. My family had much more food on the table and clothes on our backs whenever I was out and about on some adventure. As a result, I was allowed a very high level of freedom. This also contributed to the erosion of my level of discipline. Things had gotten so bad that there were times when my mother had to tie me and physically restrain me so that I would not leave home.

Between the years 1998-2000, if the police brought me home six hundred nights out of about one thousand, then I can smile and say that I was not even half as bad as people who knew me all my life would try to make me out to be. It was not that I was a bad person or a troublemaker, as a matter fact, ask anyone and they would tell you, after "Pastor Garvin" came "Smartman Garvin". I was always the smartest kid they had all ever met, maybe even to this day. The police bringing me home on an average two hundred nights of the year within those three years were for only either one of three reasons.

One of those reasons, by official request of either Prime Minister Panday, the Leader of the Opposition and former Prime Minister, Mr. Patrick Manning, as well as many other high ranking government ministers which I, for some reason or the other, gained an opportunity to win the hearts and support through that gift God gave me, which the devil was then trying to destroy.

Another reason for the police dropping me home would have been because I was either having a late night dinner by myself at some top priced, high end restaurant, ordering more food than a family of four could eat, or having a large sum of U.S. dollars and other foreign currencies in my possession. That worried a lot of genuine people who would often call the police to investigate where I got the money from. The police would then in turn take me home to my awaiting mother.

I remember eating lunch at T.G.I. Friday's around the Queen's Park Savannah one day, as I would often do, and my regular hostess Sue came with another hostess and sat down at my table. Sue explained to me that she and the other girl would normally eat together every day and out of genuine care and concern for my welfare, she continued on to tell me that both their lunches together does not cost nearly half as much as my lunch and that I really should take it down a bit and save some money. It made sense and spending less would have helped secure my future financially, but my arch enemy the devil, who roams the earth to and fro like a roaring lion seeking whom he may devour, never intended on fulfilling any promises of a good future just as in the Bible in Matthew 4:8-11,

> The devil took Jesus on an exceedingly high mountain (legend has it that it could have been a mountain in the Italian town of Ravello!) showed him all the kingdoms of the world and the glory of them and told him that he would give Jesus all these thing if he would but fall down and worship him. Jesus however, knowing that his Father in Heaven had already given all things unto him and that his Father, your Father, my Father, our Father in Heaven is the only one who is worthy of worship, replied with such authority that the devil left and never came back!

Oh how I wish that when the glory of this world was offered to me I had replied like Jesus did and would have therefore saved myself a lot of hurt and pain and suffering in life. But then again God always has a plan. He always makes a way where there seems to be none. Think about it, if I had the ability back then to withstand the pressure of the nickname my brother gave to me, then you most likely would not have been reading this story right now. True, I might have been one of God's mighty men, but this story would have been one of those ordinary everyday stories of a boy that grew up in church and loved God with his whole heart and delighted in His presence, as David was delighted and God in return blessed him with favor, wealth and grace. But that story was not to be written about my life.

Finally, the last reason as to why the police would be taking me home back to my mother would have been because of me always trying to book into some fancy hotel late at night. This little boy, all by himself once again with a huge sum of money, this always called for the police. Even the drug dealers would later on in life let me know that back then, in the wee hours of the morning, when they would see those flashing blue lights coming up the street, they would not worry because they knew it was only me coming home with my escort.

I was never in any kind of real trouble with the law. What I had was a spirit of restlessness that had me on the go all the time. I used my gifts of fast thinking and good speaking that God had given me, to make my own way through life and if anyone tried to point me to a good direction, the devil would set in and convince me to go the opposite way. I was so much trouble that one Saturday morning, my mother sent me to the nearby shop to purchase some butter and I instead took a trip to the sister island of Tobago.

I can remember exactly how it unfolded as if it were yesterday. "Garvin, go with Clifford to the shop and buy half of a butter and come directly back home" my mother said to me. She turned to her then boyfriend and said "Clifford, make sure he come straight back home, before you go down the road. Be sure to watch him, make sure he comes home."

"Garvin I'll beat you badly if you don't come home directly, you would be in big trouble! You'd better go to the shop with Clifford and come right back here and nowhere else" she yelled at me once again, handing me a five dollar bill sometime during the process. "Hmmm", my mom was so worried that I'd run off that day to go on one of my many unsafe adventures like I always do. She was so worried that her worrying excited me! "Where could I go today" was the daydream topic in my mind when she shocked me back to reality it a warning lash with a thick fake leather belt that belonged to Clifford, the guy she was living with at the time. She had plans to give me a good licking if I was to run off and come back late at night. I did not want that so I knew instantly that I would be gone all night. She did not even realize that I had opted to wear sneakers instead of slippers.

I left the house with Clifford, who was on his way to the city of Belmont, about 10 miles away from our house, 1.5 miles from Port-of-Spain, and I sure enough went directly into the shop to purchase the butter. Once I was sure he was gone, I emerged from the shop without any butter and headed the other way, off on my journey.

Wow! The island of Tobago, I made it, it was all so easy. One six hour boat ride, a ticket that cost $25.00 at the time and a little smart talk about why a small child like myself was traveling from one island to the other all alone, was all it took for me to explore another part of my country. I had seen more of it than most fifty year old natives. Now I was where hundreds of thousands had not dared to venture, Tobago!

The telephone number 639-0777 was the first thing I noticed as I exited the port. It was the delivery number for the local Scarborough KFC. Jacob's Hotel read the sign next to KFC and it was the place I figured that I should be heading. After walking a few meters up the street I came across a bar of some sort. I decided that there would be a good place to stop in and inquire about the guest house. Which group of brawling drunks would not assist a lost eleven year old boy?

The police were once again called in, but this time I had the advantage, they did not yet know me. Most of the cops in Trinidad had already come to know me, but Tobago was fresh breeding grounds. When they arrived, I told them that my uncle told me to meet him at Jacob's Guest House and that I had TT$500.00 stuck in my underwear but lost it when I was using the bathroom sometime along the boat ride. I told them his number was 639-8321 a combination of the 639 area code I saw on the wall of KFC and the 8321 was the last four digits of the telephone number to a family that loved me and took care of me. Lucky for me that number just kept on ringing so I convinced them that it meant he already left home and was on his way to Jacob's Guest House to pick me up. Unfortunately the owner of the bar was himself a relative of the Jacob family and called the guest house to inquire on behalf of the police about my uncle. They of course they had no knowledge of either of us. It was off to the station until they could figure out what to do with me.

With a smile on my face I laid on a bunk bed in the basement of the Scarborough Police Station with the off duty officers all chatting about me. They were discussing what they were going to do with me if they were unable to find my uncle who for some reason was not answering the phone. My parents put me on the boat to Tobago then they caught a plane to London, England for a two month vacation, was the story I told them. Furthermore, I did not know my uncle's address in Tobago, only his phone number and that I was in effect lost. I stared out the basement window looking at what seemed to be the port, with feelings of both delight and worry. I wondered how I ended up here again, in the hands of the police, this time with a really crazy story. Sigh, well at least I am not going home tonight, which translated into no licking for me!

The next day I was brought to the Inspector's Office. Upon my arrival to his desk, he opened a draw and took his whip out. It gave him a ripple effect which even took me by surprise. I shot both my hands into the air and said "My name is Romel Ravello, I am 11 years old, I live Upper 7th Avenue, Malick, Barataria on the island of Trinidad and I ran away from home. Please don't beat me."

In Tobago at the time, there was no official facility or organization for runaway children, so the officers took me to the Scarborough Hospital where I was warded after giving the police officers the information necessary to contact my mother for her to come get me. It was about 4:25 am the following morning that I was awoken by my mother. She was so happy that I was safe and was again within her embrace. She did not beat me, but that was only because the police inspector at the Scarborough Station made her give me a good licking before I was allowed to depart the island. I was so sore by the time I got home I slept an entire two days.

My mom would often threaten to put me into an orphanage because she could no longer handle me. I listened to no one and did whatever I felt like. Even after that Tobago experience, later that week I took a trip to the airport and attempted to board a flight heading to Dallas. This ended badly when I was discovered onboard before takeoff. I could not have taken the Airport Police officers to my mother's house mere days after she came got me on an island six hours away! So I instead took them to my grandmother's house in "Never Dirty" Morvant.

It seemed as if they stood outside of my grandmother's house and waited for the entire village to gather before giving an overly exaggerated version of what happened. They made me out to be sleek and clever when it really was just an example of how poor the security at the island's only airport was. I just walked into the airport, passed customs and boarded the plane!

Chapter VI

Fighting my Way Out, or In?

It was not even a month following both those incidents that I struck out from home and headed on my own direction in life. At the ripe old age of eleven, I left home. While I did long for the freedom and independence, the main reason I left was due to a fight that I had gotten into with an eighteen year old boy who lived a few houses away from us. I always stand true to the fact that I have never once fought in my life, even to this very day. However, this incident was very different.

Eddie, the eighteen year old, would occasionally did all sorts of horrid things to me. I remember him kicking me down a hill, punching me in the face, spitting on me and beating me up to take my money. A lot of others take advantage of me, but Eddie was different. There was something evil about him. Sometimes he would take my belongings or my money and force me to say vile things like 'I had sex with men for the money' and other offensive and degrading things. I truly hated him for what he would do to me. My brothers would not even help me because all of these guys had become their friends and they valued their friendship and entertainment more than my wellbeing.

One Saturday morning, I was on my way to the mall to buy myself a new suit and maybe some shoes if I could find some to suit my fancy. I saw him at the bottom of the hill doing some sort of work with a shovel. As I saw him, I became afraid because I had about two thousand United States dollars in my pocket which I had saved up all week long to go to the mall. As I started to walk down the hill toward Eddie's direction I saw a glass beer bottle. Something told me that I should break the head of the bottle off and take it along with me in case Eddie tried to beat me up and take away my money, then I would be able to defend myself, bad idea!

As I passed by his house, with him just about five feet away from me, it was as though I did not exist at all. I passed by so freely for the first time, that it really puzzled me. Then, my old enemy the devil stepped in and began to roar like a lion, waging war against God's plan for my life. As I walked down the road on my way to the mall having passed Eddie, a spirit of discontentment came over me and I became angry. I thought about how I was all ready to stand up to him and how he shut me down by not paying me any attention. An evil rage then entered me and like a mad bull, I reversed my direction and walked towards him. I called him out of his yard to fight but he paid me no mind. There was no gate to his yard however, so after calling out to him a few times, I decided to go in after him.

I charged into his yard at him with such wrath that one would swear I was about to beat up this towering eighteen year old. How foolish of me. He dropped his shovel and without any effort, held on to me and threw me on the ground. Eddie's sister who was sitting in the porch at the time, jumped to her feet and started screaming like crazy. I looked and my shirt and it was totally covered in blood. He grabbed hold of me and the broken bottle head which I was still holding pierced his left hand directly in line with his heart. The fight was over before it even got started.

    I never went back home after that fight, my mother opted to have me stay at the home of an aunt of mine, which to me was total freedom to do whatever I wanted. My aunt Susan was far too busy with her kids and job and life to pay much attention to me and I therefore had the freedom that I so longed for.

Chapter VII

Life in Islam

It was not long after leaving my mother's home that I enrolled myself into an Islamic boarding school for a year. I figured that it was the best way to move out and be totally on my own. I chose that school as my brother Randy, who I looked up to, had just a few months earlier converted to Islam and I wanted to follow in his footsteps. However, the God who made the world and everything in it, the Lord of heaven and earth was calling my life down a different path.

I excelled at Darul Uloom, Institute of Higher Islamic Studies and Secondary Education, just as I did in everything else that I set my mind to. God's mark was on me and no matter the situation or the circumstances; He was always there, never leaving my side, never forsaking me. For you see when God has a plan for your life, you can try to run as far away from His plan as you possibly could, but God has a way of fulfilling His plan in His perfect time. Just as Jonah, when God gave him the mission of going to the East to the people of Nineveh so that they who did not know His law, could hear of it and repent from their wicked ways and be saved. Jonah felt in his heart for some very valid reasons that it would have been better for God not to give those wicked people a chance at repentance but rather for Him to destroy the city instead.

I look back at my life and I can see that the idea of Jonah is one that is very relevant to my personal experiences. Jonah thought, like me, that if he were to run as far away in the opposite direction, then maybe God would stop telling him that He wanted him to go preach in the city of Nineveh. So Jonah took a ship and sailed away to the uttermost Western city of Tarshish.

But God! Just that in itself is probably the most profound statement since the introduction of speaking, way back when God made men. But God knew all about Jonah's plans and He sent a mighty storm that almost wrecked the ship. Jonah was asleep while this was going on and had to be awakened by the captain. After Jonah explained why the storm was occurring and what he had done, he asked them to throw him overboard so that the storm would cease. When they did throw him into the sea God had already prepared a great fish to swallow Jonah for three days and nights then spit him out. That's what it took for Jonah to say "okay God, let your will be done!" Islam was my ship ready to sail away from God's plan, but unlike Jonah I had no valid reason.

After finishing my first year of Islamic Collage and spending almost another year of three night Jamaat throughout various Masjid's on the island, I paid a visit to my brother Randy who was at the time recruited by the number two, top lieutenant of a group that could be perceived as the local Taliban and was living in one of his safe houses, just on the outskirts of the city of Port-of-Spain.

The guns, the drugs and the money all had my mouth watering, but what I really desired was the power and respect that the members of this organization had on the streets. I always had this crazy dream of walking through the capital city along the busy streets having no one bump into to me or step on my shoes. I also dreamt of fame, of everybody knowing my name. Oh, how we must be careful of the things we wish for.

It seemed to me that these brothers had the things that I wanted. I wanted it so badly that it was no surprise to anyone that before that week was over, I was recruited by the third top ranking individual of the Jamaat Al Muslimeen organization, Lincoln Alexis, better known as Salim Rasheed or "Small Salim." Yasin Abu-Bakr, the founder of the organization, expelled Small Salim just days later; for fear that he might have soon taken over the organization.

Salim treated me like his son and took me everywhere with him. I felt powerful around Salim. He was a very powerful and respected man within the island and he made everyone else respect me the same way. Once again I had the respect of the adults, but it was a respect that I almost paid for with my life. Many attempts were made on Salim's life and consequently, mine as well. Had God not wanted me alive for His purposes, I would have been dead many, many times over.

On three occasions, I was shot after at close range, once by multiple shooters but God did not allow a single bullet to touch my skin. Once, a guy stood about five feet away from me and emptied the clip of a fully automatic Mac 11. Another time, someone placed a Smith and Western 45 on my chest and squeezed the trigger, not once, but three times and the gun refused to go off. As I ran away, it suddenly started working again and he emptied the magazine behind me but it was too late, God had already delivered me.

Because of my extensive knowledge of Islam and the Quran, Salim would often allow me to lead the prayer most of the times when we guarded at a place where he was considered 'the new boss'. This caused Mark Guerra, second only to Yasin Abu-Bakr of the Jamaat Al Muslimeen, to take great notice of me and one day he asked me to come over to his house at 6:00am the following day. Once again the devil, which seemed to have already won, was about to attempt to seal his victory over my life.

I got to Mark Guerra's house at 6:23am the next day, making him a bit upset that a thirteen year old would have the nerve to not be on time to see a person as important as he was. I explained to him however that I was late because Salaat Ur Fajr was at 6:04am and I was unsure if it would have been right for me to join his family for morning pray when he had daughters that he would certainly have to lead in pray. He replied to me that unfortunately during his thirty something years of Islam, he had never once woken up himself nor his family for morning pray. He told me that I was forgiven for being late because he understood that Allah was to come first in everything. After this exchange, he then proceeded to question me as to exactly how deep my knowledge of Islam really was.

I started off by reciting what is considered the most scared chapters of the Quran, Surah Yasin. I then went on for about three uninterrupted hours basically teaching him and the two brothers he had with him about the Quran, the Hadith's, and the Sunna of their prophet Mohammad. I felt a little embarrassed after I ran out of things I knew after only a mere three hours. Mark and his two buddies on the other hand were dumbfounded. He found me to be very knowledgeable on the matter for my age and was interested in knowing what my reason behind learning so intensely was.

He turned to me and said "Akee, anything you wish to ask for is yours but I need to ask you for something as well and its very important" I told him that I needed nothing presently but was thankful for his offer and that I would be willing to facilitate any request he had to the best of my abilities. He then turned to me and said "With Allah and these two brothers present as witnesses, I have a daughter inside and she is the same age as you are. I want you to get married to her for me so that even though I wasted my chance to practice my religion, my daughter would be raised right!"

"If it was the will of God" was my modest reply. I was confused and excited at the same time. I had captivated Mark Guerra with the words of my mouth and now he wanted me to marry his daughter Jameela! After that, Mark started taking me around with him and introduced me to many of his associates, informing them that I was about to marry Jameela in five weeks' time and I would soon be his main man of business.

He took me to one of the richest communities in Trinidad, showed me a particular mansion and told me that it would now belong to me, with his daughter as my wife so I was not to worry about anything. He made me open a bank account and told me he would soon transfer twenty million dollars into it so that it would be safe.

However, there was something weird about all his sudden movements. I believe that he knew he was going to die soon and sure enough exactly three weeks after I gave him a three hour lecture on Islam, he was shot dead. But this was no work of the devil. Mark was killed during internal fighting within his gang at John-John, Laventille. Immediately following his death, many people who were members for many years, wanted to take over the top seat but in the back of their minds, they all knew that Mark had already appointed his successor mere weeks before, me!

They all knew it, so it was no surprise that at the funeral I could have felt their prying eyes all over me. Men, women and children in dark Muslim wear all watching my every move. There were guys high on top of tall graves watching down it at me. Everywhere I turned they were watching. Amazingly, I had not prayed to the one true and living God in years and I was now a professing Muslim well learned in the teaching of Islam. Yet in that cemetery while those vultures looked down on me, underneath my breath the words of the Lord came to me! Psalms 23: 4-6,

"Yeah, though I walk through the valley of the shadow of death I shall fear no evil, for Thou art with me; thy rod and thy staff they comfort me. Thou prepare a table before me in the presence of my enemies: thou anoint my head with oil; my cup overflows. Surely goodness and mercy shall follow me all the days of my life: and I will dwell in the house of the Lord forever!"

The peace that came with the word of God was so great that I forgot all about who was watching me. I was able to cast my burden unto a God that I had rejected simply because He cares for us. Unfortunately, for the rest of the day I was again attacked by the devil as he sent wave after wave of attacks against my mind. He bombarded me with his evil spirits of pride, lies, deception, and the like. By the time I left the cemetery after praying to the Lord Jesus, I was so puffed by the stupid, egotistic idea that everyone was actually showing me a lot of respect and not hate!

Later, I was dumb enough to visit Mark's house to pay my personal respects to his family and explain to his wife Beverly that I would understand if it was not her wish to have me marry her young daughter now that her husband was no longer alive. When I got to John John later that evening, I did not even get the chance to reach the front gate before being approached by a group of common thugs claiming that I was the one responsible for Mark death. Their logic was that for the past three weeks, I was always with him no matter where he went, and if I for some reason was not present with him he would have no doubt told me exactly where he was going. Therefore, when they saw him drop me off at his house mere hours before he was killed, he would have indeed told me that he was on his way to his farm in Wallerfield, a small town about thirty miles to the East of the Port-of-Spain where Mark lived. As a result, they insisted that I had to be the tip off guy for Mark's ambush.

They were about to kill me right then and there and the only word that could have come to my lips was "Jesus" and how reassuring it is when you know that there is supernatural power in the name of Jesus! For as the word ensued softly from my lips, a band of police officers, expecting trouble on such a night, turned the corner and were just a few meters away. The unexpecting young men all froze and the police continued their walk towards the main road. Immediately, without saying a word to anyone, I continued to walk alongside them. God had yet again spared my life. It was a thing that He would have often had to do in my life growing up as a young, poor, hopeful, adventurous and intelligent boy in an island such as Trinidad in the West Indies.

Fear infected my body after this incident. I feared everyone that was associated with the Jamaat Al Muslimeen. I was even too afraid of returning to the house I lived in with Salim Rasheed and his family. I trusted no one and choose instead to sleep on the sidewalks of the back streets of the other end of the island, in the southern city of San Fernando.

Chapter VIII

Fighting my Fate

For two months when I was about fourteen years old, I slept on the streets of that southern city before I came to my senses and called Salim who told me to come to Port-of-Spain and meet him. When I got there, we then went to Carenage, to the house of Kasim Rasheed, another expelled member of the Jamaat Al Muslimeen. We stayed there for almost a year because there were bounties on both the heads of Salim and Kasim as well as another brother named Zaakie.

The three was expelled from the Jamaat Al Muslimeen for fear of an uprising against Abu-Bakr but Salim as the main target, the leader of the suspected rebellion to come, the new Imam. There was already a serious attack on his life months earlier when he was shot several times outside the very popular movie theater MovieTowne. Even though this event had a profound impact on my life I don't see the need to go into the details of it as I was not present at the time. I did however spend his entire hospital stay right there with him, watching over him and protecting him in my own little way. I was willing to eliminate any treat whatsoever that may have arisen whilst Salim was in the hospital, he was like my father.

After spending about a year at Kasim's house, I had a falling out with Salim and decided to branch off on my own once again. I had been smoking marijuana for about two years by then and it was slowly messing up by brain. Salim picked up on this one day and told me that I could no longer smoke because it was not right for him to allow me, a fifteen year old boy, to smoke illegal drugs.

In the usual way that I adopted over the years, I ranted and raved telling Salim that he had no right telling me that I should not smoke the ganja. To me it seemed hypocritical. I asked him why during the day he was telling me about the ill effects of smoking marijuana and then at night, we would be the ones either on Kasim's or Salim's speed boats going to neighbouring Venezuelan waters to exchange food and cash for drugs, guns and ammunition.

While I was saying these things to him, I was at the same time tossing my clothing into a garbage bag shouting that I had enough and was leaving. He told me that I was only "a harden kid" that won't listen and that this time I was not going anywhere. He turned to another there at the house and told him "If Yasar (as he opted to call me after his fallout with Abu-Bakr) tries to cross the boundary line shoot him in the leg!" I paid no attention to this order that he gave because I knew in my heart that he would stand it down as I approached the boundary line. He loved me, I was like his son. I would be with him anywhere he went and if I was not present with him, he was most likely doing something really bad and did not want me there.

That order to shoot, ha! It would have been a sure thing if it was anybody else, but my Father in heaven caused him to view me as his son and spared my life. A "blood in blood out" organization and I got in without spilling blood, and was seemingly out without doing the same. "God granted me favor like He granted Joseph, sparing his life by causing his brothers to sell him off to a foreign people heading to a foreign land." But when Joseph got there, God granted him so much favor that he became basically the general manager of the then superpower nation, Egypt.

There is always something special that happens that lets you know that God is at work in your situation. I left there safely and headed east to the town Sangre Grande, to the house of one of Salim's associates, a guy that I have only known as "Rope." I spent about two weeks with Rope and his crew a few weeks earlier to teach and encourage them towards converting to Islam. However, I was fed up with being the star teacher and then once again in some strange way, in a totally different religion, I felt like I was Pastor Garvin and I was again resentful of that. Rope was disappointed but still believed in my ability to inspire the youths towards a better way of life through devotion to Allah.

When I left Kasim's house and got to Sangre Grande, I was well received by the gang there despite the fact that Rope was not present. I was allowed to go into his house to refresh myself and take a rest. Rope got home a few hours later and was very pleased to find me at his residence. He told me that I would always have my own room at his house and that it was available to me whenever I wanted to come. He then invited me outside to smoke a few joints with him the boys.

While out in the street smoking with Rope, his uncle and about four other members of his gang, Rope's cell phone rang, it was Salim. About one hour after I stormed out of Kasim's house, the police executed a search warrant finding several guns and arresting everyone present except himself and Kasim, as they are deemed too powerful to touch. After speaking with Salim for about five minutes Rope then mentioned that I came to his house with my clothing and he had offered me shelter. As the conversation continued, Rope started looking at me differently and made me very uncomfortable. Suddenly he called one of his boys and quietly sent him for something in the bushes behind the house. By this time, I was so scared and was relieved when Rope's uncle called me aside and asked me to walk over to his house to help him with something.

As we got to his house, he informed me that he suspected that my life was in danger. He gave me some money and told me to run away. So I ran, I ran as fast as my skinny legs would carry me. I ran to the

Eastern Main Road and flagged down a maxi-taxi and headed to the community that my family had shared that horrible two room apartment almost a decade earlier, Laventille Road, Febeau Village, San Juan. I was welcomed into the house of a former crime boss nicknamed Ken-man. Every one respected me around there since I was a little boy so I felt quite at home amongst them for about two weeks until one evening I saw a familiar S500 Mercedes Benz coming up the one way in, one way out, street that is Laventille Road. It was Salim Rasheed.

"But how could this be?" I pondered. I choose Laventille Road as my safe haven because the gang there was at war with the Jamaat Al Muslimeen and essentially Islam as a whole. Many lives were lost in this war so one did not tolerate the other at all. As such, it was a complete surprise to me when Salim pulled up and shook hands with Cojo the leader of the Laventille Road gang.

When Cojo asked me when I first got to Laventille Road what my situation was, I told him that Salim Rasheed wanted me dead and I needed protection. The people of Laventille Road were regarded as one and if you were from there, they would not allow outsiders to mess with you. Little did I know that Salim was originally from San Juan and he was a childhood friend of Cojo. He told Cojo that it was ludicrous for a boss of his stature to be out gunning for a young boy like myself, especially after considering me as his own son for such a very long time.

He told Cojo that I was disrespectful and listened to no one and it would be best for him to make me leave the neighborhood. Cojo then turned to me, slapped me in the face and told me to leave the area. Salim stayed behind, talking to Cojo and once again I had no place to live. This time I was officially a street child.

Chapter IX

You Really Can't Imagine the Abuse

I left San Juan and walked a many miles to the capital city wandering the streets for hours not knowing where I was going to rest my head. To make matters worse it started raining. I was invited to shelter the rain inside the empty Salvatory Building by the lone male security officer working there that dreadful January 2004 night. It was the second time, in my innocent childhood, that I was sexually assaulted.

I never disclosed the details of the first assault until recently during the course of writing the book. Furthermore I ask that you please forgive me but I honestly do not wish to go into the details of this experience at this time. Making matters worse, a storm was about to hit Trinidad. After surviving the brutality of the storm I was left to roam the streets. Sleeping on sidewalks, park benches, abandoned vehicles and wherever I could get to lay my head down. I lived mainly on the bits of edibles that people might throw out, things one would find in a trashcan.

My experiences living on the streets are far too numerous to go into full detail about. I need you only to trust me when I say that no child should endure even some of the more pleasant things I went through between the ages of 13-15. Things that, had it not been for the love of my personal Lord and Savior Jesus Christ, I would never even want to remember.

I was sexually abused by a lot of older men. Not once, not twice but three times. On one of these nights, I was sleeping in Victoria Square, a park in the capital city, when I was woken up by a group of six men who took me and held me for over a week. I was made a sex slave to their sick pleasure and even their financial gain. The pain and sense of hopelessness was overwhelmingly devastating. I remember thinking one day after being beaten, threatened and finally released, as to whether I could go on living anymore. Was life really worth it? I suffered through the days and then it happened again. It was not as physically bad as it was the first time, but mentally worst. I was left with no one to turn to nowhere to go.

I was so heartbroken and mentally exhausted by this time that I started to just go along with whatever afflictions that came my way. I was robbed by the local thugs whenever I had a little money, ill-treated by most persons who I sought help from. I was rejected, beaten, spat upon and altogether wronged. Having been through so much, it seemed as if I forgot that I had a Father in heavenly places. For many years, it did not dawn on me that there was a God sitting on the throne and all I had to do was to cry out to Him and He would have delivered me out of all of my troubles. Going through life all alone, I endured countless sufferings.

Chapter X

Welcome to Woodbrook

In mid-2004, I got a job as a busboy at the local nightclub, 51 Degrees. Even though I was only fifteen years old, I was allowed to work because I knew Joe Perez, one of the shareholders for many years. In fact, he was the very first businessman I knew. Back when I was merely eight years old I would wash the panel vans for his company Caribbean Chemicals. They did not even interview me for the job.

I also started sleeping in an abandoned house on Woodford Street, Newtown, Port of Spain. It was a house that some of the local thugs had taken control over. They allowed me to stay in, with the idea that I might join them in their illegal activities. Incidentally, I might have, had God not provided me with my first real job. I worked the night of the grand opening and was fired the very next day. Jorge, the Human Resource Manager, was experiencing some problems within his marriage and decided that the entire staff under him had to listen to these personal problems. I however refused and was immediately fired for insubordination.

When Joe heard this a week later, he in turn fired the two car park attendants and gave me the job of operating both the main parking lot and the basement parking. Parking cars was exactly where God wanted to place me at that point in time and from there on, He caused my prosperity to increase rapidly.

So here I was, parking the cars of all the rich and famous people of my island. The businessmen and women, the sporting heroes, the entertainment superstars. This was the place to be for locals and foreigners alike when one sought out nightlife in Trinidad. Everybody who was somebody and those who wanted to be somebody, all came and partied often at 51 Degrees. They would all befriend me with the hope of me reserving them a parking spot whenever they came by. Unfortunately a few months later, I was wrongfully accused of keying a customer's car and lost my job at the nightclub. However, I kept on parking cars on my own around that area for many years.

Furthermore, things started to go downhill again when the house that I was illegally living in was purchased and torn down. I was back to square one, living on the street at the age of fifteen. I felt different now though, I had more hope now than I ever had. I was connected to so many people now, I felt in my heart that one of those beautiful rich girls would certainly like me and all of my problems would be over. I switched up my dress code once more, returning to dress shoes, straight fitted jeans and slim fitted shirts. I would always try to look like a well put together, acceptable young man that a girl would be happy to take home and introduce to her parents as the love of her life.

My plan seemed so close to becoming my reality that at one time I had five different well off girls. The most beautiful one of all was a young lady from Australia. She had to have been at least 22 years old at the time. She took me home to her upscale condo one weekend in September and I could have envisioned my new life with her. She told me that her job was sending her away for a week and she would bring me back clothes, shoes and everything else I desired and that we would spend a lot of time together when she got back. I couldn't wait for this, then all of a sudden the very worst thing that could have happened to me, happened! It's the thing that I will never forget as long as I live.

Chapter XI

Scarred for Life

On Sunday September 26th 2004, I was just opposite the United States Embassy at West Queens Park Savannah, the very same Savannah where I slept with my family about eleven years earlier. I finished parking cars outside the night club Saturday night and was asleep on a bench. This was when one unknown person walked up to me, poured acid on my face and ran away.

I jumped up out of my sleep screaming frantically, charging around like a mad bull. I rubbed my face in the grass to no relief, then in the dirt and the drain. I remember running around in a circle screaming aloud "What have you done to me!!? What have you done!?" The feeling still is indescribable, to this day. The best picture I can give is to ask you to imagine a pot of water bubbling under intense heat. Now try to imagine if you can, that being skin and flesh boiling and exploding into bubbles like that.

All of my panicking took about three or four minutes of eternity and finally I calmed myself down. I opened my eyes just enough to peek through and see a phone booth about twenty meters away. I ran to it and called the police emergence hotline, 999. A female officer answered the phone and as calm as I possibly could have, I told her what happened. She in turned dispatched an ambulance to come get me as I pleaded with her not to hang up the phone. I begged her to stay on the line whilst the ambulance was making their way to me. She was indeed gracious enough to grant me my request in spite of the many other emergency calls that would have been coming in. I thank God for that officer! I thank Him that she did not say to me that she had done her job and had to hang the phone up, for surely I do not know what might have happened to me had she not stayed on the line that morning. As soon as the ambulance arrived some five minutes later, they placed me inside of the van and I passed out.

I woke up when we arrived at the Port of Spain General Hospital and remember opening my eyes from time to time. I was forced to shut them however due to the looks of shock and horror that I kept seeing on the faces of all those I rolled past. They took me inside and rushed me directly into the operating room, again I passed out.

On Wednesday 29th I awoke warded at the hospital, still uncertain of exactly what happened. All I knew was that I went to sleep, woke up in absolute pain and now my entire head was bandaged up. The distress that awoke me, with that burning and indescribable pain, showed the absence of God in the hearts of men. I had no family, no friends.

I asked one of the nurses what happened and she told me that someone had thrown acid on my face and that I would never look the same again. Upon hearing this, my heart shattered. I was homeless and had just lost the only thing I thought would have been able to get me off the streets, "my good looks." After the nurse left I got up, went to the washroom, took the bandages off my face and looked in the mirror. My first reaction was that the thing in the mirror was not human. It looked like a monster and then I realized that thing in the mirror was me. In a mad rage I ran from the hospital.

I ran out the front gate and headed north up the street, back to the Queens Park Savannah. As I got to the middle of the open field, I dropped to my knees and cried out to God for the first time in many years. I prayed and asked Him to show up once more in my life. I asked him to prove Himself mighty and burst the heavens open and with His own hand crush me, end my life and finally allow ease of pain by way of the grave. I asked him to save me any further hardship that this thing called life had to offer to me. I laid out there in the open field crying for about three hours. When God refused to answer my cry for death, I made up my mind that I wanted nothing to do with God.

I utterly rejected Him and in my rebellion within my own heart, I debunked the very notion that a Supreme Being existed, far less an all loving, all knowing, and all powerful God who is in control of every situation. "Where was He when I needed Him the most as a young boy?" I thought. He was not there and therefore cannot exist. It's amazing how we quite often forget all the good things God has done for us in the past whenever He does not show up when we think He ought to have showed up.

I thank God that now I understand that we, unaware of His ultimate plan for our life, have no right to question when and why He chooses to intervene in our lives. He was working it out all for His glory at His perfect timing!

Chapter XII

Suicide on my Mind

Life was much harder now more than ever before, it took me at least six months before I was brave enough to start back parking cars again. Suicide thoughts deliberated in my mind daily. I decided that if I survived until Carnival, I would end my life after that.

There was something special about Trinidad and Tobago Carnival. You just could not miss this two day festival. It truly is unlike any other festival in the world. The reason for that is simple, Trinidad Carnival is Bacchanal! Now for me to explain our Carnival, my country's national festival, I must first explain what is bacchanal because "Carnival is Bacchanal".

Bacchanal stems from the Latin word Bacchanalia: A festival of Bacchus celebrating the Greek god of wine, Dionysus. It entailed intoxication, revelry, uninhibited ecstasy and all of the pitfalls that go with this. Everything that was ancient Latin Bacchanalia, is present in Trinidad Carnival. It is as if the spirit of Dionysus himself would descend on my island, plant his feet on the Queen's Park Savannah and lure people to go crazy with their sensual dancing (wining, as it is called in Trinidad and Tobago), drinking and partying for weeks on end.

To some, the only time of the year that one can have to truly break loose and be free to enjoy all the lustful and sinful pleasures that life has to offer, all climaxes on Carnival Monday and Tuesday in a brilliantly degrading display of bikinis, feathers, beads, rum and music all in the blazing hot sun. Parading down the streets wining and gyrating to the rhythm of some of the most vulgar and morally disgraceful music that you will ever hear in your life! Yes this is the splendor, the magnificence, the glory of Trinidad and Tobago Carnival and I was right smack in the middle of it.

I would know when the carnival season was about to kick off when that beautiful tractor would pull into Adam Smith Square early in the morning every year. "The lovely yellow tractor was once again here to save me!" was the first thought that followed the big smile and jolly glow that emanated from my face as I turned in my bed. My bed at that time would be one of the benches in that very same Adam Smith Square, the ones with the pieces of iron along the center.

That tractor was however, my once a year five star hotel. Complete with shelter from the elements, a very soft chair that reclines and spins around as well as much needed privacy. But carnival meant so much more, it meant parties all over Woodbrook. Most of the promoters of these parties I knew, so I would either be partying for free, working in the party or parking cars. Any which way, I was having a lot of fun and making good money whenever carnival came around. I remember 'chipping' (dancing) around the savannah Carnival Tuesday afternoon and suddenly deciding to go for a 'wine' on a girl. Not considering that I had just came out of hiding for almost six months because of the extent of the disfiguration of my face and neck, I approached this girl for a dance from behind to the music of Machel Montano. For the first two seconds she seemed delighted and decided to look back to see who she was dancing with. The pleasant smile on her face turned into a look of horror at once when she saw my face. Her scream overshadowed even the loudest music playing. She screamed and ran as if she had just come face to face with the most hideous and dreadful monster in existence. I in return attempted to play it cool by pretending that nothing happened, but as I turned and danced away, my mind was made up that I had no more to live for and it was time for me to die.

Carnival for me was over when suddenly a hand wrapped around my shoulder and someone was embracing and jumping up with me. I looked to my left and to my utter amazement, it was Sir Brian Charles Lara. World Record holding bat's man and undisputedly the greatest cricketer to have ever lived. He is like what Michael Jordan is to basketball, Lionel Messi to Soccer, or Bob Marley to music. He was by far the most famous person from my country and he was jumping with me for carnival. Oh what a joyful time it was indeed.

We stuck together for about half of an hour and for that timeframe I was somehow allowed to forget all of my problems. For when people looked at me, it was not my burnt face that they saw. All they saw was that Brian Lara was standing right next to me and we were moving together! Later on in life, the Lord revealed to me that He Himself had sent Brian Lara to me so that I might enjoy myself and forget any thoughts about ending my life. Not that God condoned any of the activities taking place, but that was maybe the only way for Him to reach me.

You see, I'm from an island where if you don't look absolutely perfect then something has to be wrong with you, so at that point in time to people, Brian Lara was the most perfect being to be around and God used him to boost my self-esteem. He reassured me that there were still people in the world that would accept me for who I was on the inside and not whatever I looked like on the outside.

I was strengthened for days after this, which turned into weeks and as the weeks rapidly turned into months, I started to develop a "Don't Care" mentality. I pretended not to care about the stares and the jeers, the laughs and the insults. I acted as if it did not bother me at all, but everyone knew it did. However this eventually eroded and after some time, I went about cursing everybody out and would daily break down into tears in the streets. The continued treatment of disregard by my fellow countrymen resulted in me falling back into depression.

Taxis would not pick me up, neither would buses. Everywhere I had to go, I had to walk and walk back. Sometimes a taxi would stop and when I opened the door, the driver would get a good look at me and then they would speed off. Being halfway outside the car, I would always fall flat on the ground. If a driver happened to pick me up, then other passengers in the car would threaten to exit the taxi if the driver did not put me out at once. They claimed that I was no longer human, that I was a monster and that they would have bad dreams at night on my account.

"Let everything that has breath praise the Lord" says the Holy Scriptures. I could go on no longer without praising His Holy name! The ways in which He directly stepped in multiple times and with His mighty hand, intervened and saved my life from the many attempts that was made on me by others and more so, attempts made by myself. There was a restaurant and bar located on Cipriani Blvd which I frequented just about every day for the months that I was in Woodbrook prior to my incident in September. I had not been there since being so horridly disfigured however. As I entered the front door, a well to do, East Indian woman sitting at the table closest to the door, heard the squeak that the hinges of the door made and in her curiousness or as we say in Trinidad "fastness" while chewing on her roti, she turned to see who was coming through the door. My eyes caught hers and for a split second, I could have seen her absolute disgust of my appearance. The look in her eyes felt as hot and sizzling as though a bullet had hit my heart. I held my chest as I gasped for a single breath of air in between the multitude of tears that immediately flowed freely and uncontrollably down my face. I only saw her for a split second because as she looked me in the face that was all that it took for her to start screaming and at once began to throw up the roti she was eating!

The owner rushed over to me yelling and screaming at me to get out as if I was robbing the store or beating a customer. If photos were taken of the commotion in the restaurant that day, you would think that I had a gun and was holding everyone hostage. You would never suspect that all I did was walk through the door. Following that, I was not allowed to enter into most of the restaurants in my community. They would chase me off like a dog. They would run me like I was a monster.

Most of the international franchises however, would treat me almost just as they would treat any other customer. They would most likely politely suggest a seat somewhere in a corner or close to the back. TGI Friday's was much different. I was indeed just another customer at that establishment. I had been eating there since I was a little boy and most of the employees knew me from over the years. The only issue was that TGI was one the most expensive restaurants on the island.

I would sleep in Adam Smith Square, wake up and go across the street and sit in front of Republic Bank and beg for money. When I figured that I had enough to eat lunch at TGI Friday's then I would head to Cipriani Boulevard where I would take a shower at the house of Ms. Cheryl Ifill then it was off to lunch. Later on in the day I would park cars along the side of the street until I again had enough money and I was off again once more to TGI Friday's for dinner. This was my daily routine for years, it was truly the only place I could have gotten real humane treatment.

But life in general was miserable. I hated living and I cursed everyone, every day. Even those that would give me money daily I had no regard for. I appreciated nothing and no one. I was totally unconcerned with everything and finally I had foolishly totally convinced myself that there was no God. No God, no heaven, no hell, this life was all there was to look forward to and heaven and hell was right here in this life on earth.

I weighed in the balance that I had a few moments in heaven throughout a life time of hell and had purposed in my heart from that point on that I did not want to live this life any longer. I made my mind up that Romel Ravello should no longer exist!

One day not very long after as I stood Tony Roma's Restaurant and Bar on Cipriani Boulevard around noon, I kept saying in my mind "there was no God and no heaven and no hell. This life is all there is. I do not want to live this life!" As I was saying this over and over in my mind, as the tears freely flowed down my cheeks and I could make no other sound except for a soft squeal of agony and pain, people passing by would see me and cross onto the other side of the road to walk.

I glanced to my right and saw an 'NP' truck coming up the street. It must have been about 350 meters away when I first glanced at it speeding through the amber colored traffic light at the corner of Cipriani Boulevard and Tragarete Road, coming at about 90 miles per hour in my direction. My whole life flashed before my eyes and in two seconds, my mind was made up that this was going to be my escape from this world, its pain, its suffering and its cruel torment.

I could see that red and black 14-wheeler truck hitting my body and ending all of my pain. I purposed in my heart that I would not want to feel pain so I waited until the truck came to a distance where I knew the truck would hit me and I would feel absolutely nothing, it would be an instant death. I said it once more "there's no God, no heaven, no hell, this life is all there is, I do not want to live this life!" and as that gas carrier truck got within ten feet of me, I ran out into the middle of the road, closed my eyes and spread my arms wide open as if I were embracing death itself.

In a second I began to hear the brakes of the truck violently screeching along the asphalt road. I could then smell in my nostrils the scent of what appeared to be the oil from the engine and suddenly I opened my eyes and the truck was smack dead in front of my face, its front bumper brushing against my jeans. My mouth opened and the only thing I could have cried out was "my God! My God! My God!" In a mad haste, the driver jumped out of his truck and began bawling and looking underneath and behind the truck believing that he would find my lifeless body lying below there somewhere. He was in utter disbelief to find me in front of the truck completely unharmed.

He could not have explained how it was possible that the truck, going at such a high speed, was able to stop in such a short distance. The only and rightful thing he could have done was praise God in heaven that he was not the cause of my death. As for me, I was furious. I hated the name of God all the more and I felt as if He had cheated me out of what I thought was going to be my happiness, death. My anger lead to a greater disbelief in His existence, even though I could not truly believe such foolishness in my heart, knowing full well how real He had already proven Himself to be in my early childhood years.

Chapter XIII

Friends along the Way

Following this futile attempt at suicide, I reluctantly continued my car parking hustle. Many people took pity on my situation and helped me with just about anything I needed or wanted. In spite of everything, there were still so many people who lovingly cared for my wellbeing over the years. When I was a little boy, there were people like Jennifer Abraham and her husband Colin Borde, Cheril-Lynn Chambers of HOTT 93.5fm, PM Basdeo Panday, Carlos John, Kathryn Kerzanjon, Joe Pries, Wade of Auto Trim Ltd., Dave Boodoo of Autorama and many others who also added towards my development in some way or the other.

Nevertheless, my life even from back then was destined to take the course it took and I have learnt now that we should never attempt to question God as to why things which we can't explain happen. I have learnt to just trust that He knows best and He is in control of all things, working out every situation for His purpose.

Throughout my teenage and young adult life, even whilst living on the streets, I got a lot of assistance. Many people came to my aid and my defense. People such as Brian Lara, Jules Sobion, Raj Maharaj and his little brother Narindra as well as his brothers-in-law Shawn and Jessie Sammy, Mrs. Hermia Tyson-Cuffie, Mrs. Joan Yuille-Williams, Dwayne

Bravo, Machel Montano, Brook Potter, Kerwin Narine, Hayden Gill, Trevor Luke, Jason Williams, David Stone, Victor Sooknarine, PM Patrick Manning and a great deal of others whose names I cannot all remember. Some of whose names I do not even know, but in no way do I undermine their contribution to my life. There was a time in my life, not too long ago, that I honestly did not know what it really meant to have pure gratitude but I do now! Even the very same restaurant owner on Cipriani Boulevard became one of the persons that became a friend along the way.

Once upon a time saying thank you was merely meaningless words rolling out of my mouth. I had no reverence for the giver and most times did not even appreciate the gift. I was as unthankful as they came. You could have given me something or done me some good service and when asked if I was grateful, most times I would bluntly say that I was grateful for nothing, so my answer is no, I'm not!

In my present state of life however, I have learnt firstly to be thankful to my Lord Jesus Christ for dying for me so that I now have life, then He taught me to be thankful for the other good gifts He gave me and for the gifts that were given to me by my fellow men. Over powering all of this is the fact that He taught me to also be thankful for my troubles and the hardships I endured in life, for had it not been for my tremendous hardships and my many troubles, I most certainly would not have allowed him to reveal His glory in my life.

Oh yes! I am indeed thankful to all of the people and organizations that God used throughout my life to help me along the way. Those past, present and those who He will in the future send. To every person that attempted to treat me as a normal human being and even more, a friend, I am thankful to all.

There are some that were extremely outstanding in their support towards my adolescent years. Mrs. Hermia Tyson-Cuffie, who served as the Deputy Permanent Secretary in the Ministry of Community Development, Culture and Gender Affairs was one such person. I was introduced to her by the then Minister, Mrs. Joan Yuille-Williams after Prime Minister Patrick Manning gave me a "triangle card" addressed to the Minister. Mrs. Tyson-Cuffie was given the duty of organizing all of my school supplies for Islamic Boarding School.

For twelve years after that first introduction, Mrs. Tyson-Cuffie assisted me like I was her adopted son. She took me home to her mother's house to have Christmas lunch with the family. She fed me when I was hungry. She was the key player in my educational opportunities. She also had a major part in me being the only other registered resident at La Fantisie Road in St. Anns, Port-of-Spain, the Official Residence and Diplomatic Center of the Prime Minister of the

Republic of Trinidad and Tobago. I am truly grateful for all of the help Mrs. Tyson-Cuffie granted to me over the years.

Further to this, the friendship of Jules Sobion is by far without measure. I met Jules when I was working for the nightclub 51 Degrees. Back then he was driving a Honda Civic with plates that read PBP 49. He was just this skinny, tall, dark skin, dreadlocked guy that was so cool, humble and easy going. It did not take long for me to find out that he was the man behind the Julius Caesar Entertainment Company, an up and coming party promoting company that held several events annually. In the car parking business, the next biggest and related hustle that was sought after was the "Flier Gigs". Soon I was being paid by Jules to distribute fliers for his and other parties to the cars outside the nightclub, a job I took great pride in. This was not so much that I was passing out fliers, but more so the person who I was passing out the fliers for.

Within a year of dealing with Jules, he invited me to his house in the well to do gated community of Flagstaff, St. James. We hung out for a few hours and he even gave me some of the best clothes and shoes that he had in his collection at that point in time after which he dropped me back to Cipriani Boulevard where he first picked me up. Maybe to him it was nothing, but I know that my God sent Jules Sobion into my life back then so that whenever I felt sad and down, whenever I was depressed and lonely, I was able to call him and be treated as an esteemed friend. One who he was happy and proud to bring along wherever he was going and to be around whomever he was with. Jules even permanently placed my name on the guest list for all of his events which helped a lot with my social development. I was getting out more often and people were seeing me more and more, most times in the spotlight!

Friends brought friends and one night as I was parking cars, I had the esteemed honour of meeting Raj Maharaj, son-in-law to the General Contracting tycoon, Junior Sammy. Raj rolled into the basement parking lot in a black, two door, sport-model CL55 AMG Benz and instantly tipped me a one hundred dollar bill. Countless times since that first night and to this day, Raj has been there for me whenever I needed him and then a lot more times than that.

I remember this one time and I hope he does too, I was so broke and hungry on a Sunday which happened to be a public holiday, meaning that on Monday everywhere would be closed, I was in the ghetto of Belmont, on Car Street to be exact. I called Raj and told him my situation, that I had neither food nor money to survive the two days, he in turn asked me where I was. I told him where and that I would be willing to walk a distance of about one and a half miles to meet him on Cipriani Boulevard, a much safer location as months earlier an attempt to kidnap him was made. Instead, he told me to stay where I was and that he would call me when he was close by. When he called, I walked only a block away and met him on Jerningham Avenue where he gave me US$100.00, equivalent TT$600.00!

Another night he invited me to his house for one of the local festivals. I remember there was this one security at 51 Degrees, Ancil, who would give me a lot of trouble to operate my car parking services as I was no longer working for the club, but rather hustling cars on the side of the road. Well, I was at Raj's house, sitting on the couch in his living room, playing a video game with his brother Narindra, when Ancil walked in. He was in utter shock and disbelief to see me, of all people, invited to this esteemed gathering. Needless to say, he did not give me anymore trouble after that night. Raj even made him give me a ride back home to Woodbrook. Talk about favor from above!

There are many, many more things that Raj, Jules and others have done for me and if I were to try to write them all down, this book would be never ending. All I can say is thank you God for putting them in my life and placing in their hearts, the assistance and good gifts they gave to me, for we all very well know that all good gifts come from the Lord our God.

Another person I remember helping me along the way was Mrs. Marilyn King-Jack who at the time worked at the Republic Bank on the corner of Ariapita Avenue and Murray Street. I used to sit in front of the bank and beg every morning and Mrs. King-Jack along with some other employees, took it upon themselves to assist in getting me off of the streets. They contacted a local home for boys managed by Ms. Judy Rampersad who agreed to take me in. At nineteen years old, it was so exciting to have a soft, warm bed for the first time in years. There were boys my age, my peers to socialize with, games to play and more food than I could have eaten. It started off very nice at Marion House, very nice indeed, but that did not last very long. In many ways my short stay at Marion House was a very helpful and productive one.

Ms. Rampersad helped me to get enrolled at Elder's Classes where I studied O' Level English, Social Studies, Principles of Business, Principles of Accounting and Economics for ten months before writing the United Kingdom based O'Level exams. From the very first week of classes I realized that accounting was not something I was interested in and when the examination results finally came out in August 2008, I was not surprised to find out that I passed all of my subjects excepting Accounts.

While at Marion House, I also had the opportunity to attend at the same time the technical college, Servol. Mr. Joseph, an instructor at Marion House was also a teacher at Servol and one night he spoke to me about the courses offered there. I was particularly interested in their I.T. program but what really had me wanting to go was their Public Speaking

Competition. This was a competition that the school held in which the winner was awarded one year of free tuition at the school to pursue any program they desired.

"I'm going to win that competition Mr. Joseph" I said to him that very night. "It's not that easy" he replied "there will be many kids going after that title, what makes you think you would even be accepted into the competition far more to win the thing?" To this I firmly said "The difference between me and the rest of competitors is that they want to win but I have to win. I cannot afford to pay my way through school so I will have to win."

Needless to say, I was selected to compete and delivered a brilliant speech with full confidence in myself. At the end, I walked away with a trophy and one full year of free schooling, I had won the competition just as I had purposed in my heart to do. Unfortunately, like many other things I did not complete the course and therefore never graduated.

Socially, I was at the time experiencing one of my biggest meltdowns as Ms. Judy Rampersad convinced herself that despite the fact that I was a top student at both schools even with limited academic experience, that I was mentally unfit to remain living at Marion House and that it would be in my best interest for her to check me into the local mental institute, the St. Anns Mental Hospital. I attempted to refuse to go for a psychiatric evaluation because I did not believe this was necessary, but when she threatened to throw me back out onto the streets I was inclined to go along.

The medical doctor concluded that I was very intelligent for one thing and that all of my mental faculties seemed to be in check. He ruled that I was in no way a danger to society and those closest around me. Ms. Rampersad however, insisted that the hospital kept me for a week or two for further examinations. The doctor informed her that his evaluation was good enough and that the hospital would not be able to keep me without my consent, which of course I refused to give and the good doctor dismissed us. As we got back to her Toyota Yaris, Ms. Rampersad informed me that I would have to pick up my belongings as soon as we got back to Marion House, I was no longer allowed to stay there. Back on the streets once again.

Nevertheless, my education continued and with the help of Mrs. Hermia Tyson-Cuffie. My schooling at Elder's Classes was paid for by the Ministry of Community Development, Culture and Gender Affairs. She also campaigned for me to take up lodging at a boarding facility the Ministry had at #1 La Fantisie Road in St. Anns, just outside the gates to the Official Residence of the Prime Minister of the Republic of Trinidad and Tobago. After passing four out of five O'Level subjects, I moved on to the A'Level subjects of Law, Economics and Business Studies.

After passing my A'Level subjects, I worked as a Clerical Assistant in the office of the Director of Public Prosecutions, a branch of the Ministry of Legal Affairs. Following this I was enrolled into the University of the West Indies where I started pursuing my legal career at the Open Campus. I did not last more than two months at University before realizing that I did not yet have the psychological readiness that was associated with being a university student. As such I dropped out and as soon as I did this, the Ministry decided that I could no longer keep my accommodation. Yup, it was back on the street for me yet again. I did not go back into school until years later when I started working for Victor Sooknarine.

To every one person that was treating me good however, there were at least fifty that were trying to make me feel like there was no reason to continue living.

Chapter XIV

You Can't Die!

Sitting in an alley one dark, cold and lonely night in 2008, I was angry, depressed and hating everyone who had someone to turn to and somewhere to go. Hating my situation , I looked up to the sky and saw the answer. There was a ¾ inch iron pipe running from one building to the next. I climbed onto the chair I was sitting on, took my t-shirt off and tore it into a long strip of cloth. I tied one end around that iron pipe and fashioned the other into a noose around my neck. I took a deep breath, exhaled calmly for a final time and then with a smirk on my face, I extended my arms outwards and stepped off the chair.

Unknowingly, in that alley where I sat crying my heart out, there sat also another man. Hayden Gill or Bubbles as he was better known, sat low on the ground in the deep thickness of the night. He had most likely taken a few hits on his crack pipe moments before I walked into the alley and was totally zoned out, numbed up and muted. I later on came to learn that when Bubbles smoked crack cocaine from his pipe, he would freeze up with the most horrid look on his face as if he had seen a ghost. He was so silent that I did not have the slightest clue that he was within inches from where I myself sat, even so close that I would not doubt that some of the tears that flowed freely down my face may have landed on his feet.

My feet dangled in the air as the noose tighten around my neck with my heartbeat rapidly accelerating. I could slowly feel life escaping my lungs, every vein in my body was tightening, swollen and began to feel like there was fire running through them. My eyes began to roll to the back of my head just as I was ready to give up my ghost. Then suddenly, rising out of the darkness of the shadows, was the figure of a strong, muscular, bearded man who grabbed hold of my legs and began to push me upwards so that the make-shift noose around my neck would slacken.

I kicked and yelled at him, begging him to leave me alone and allow me to die in peace. In reply, fighting for breath while fighting with me to keep me alive he said to me "You cannot die, you cannot die yet! God as a plan for your life, do not give up yet!" After struggling for a minute or two and realizing that this man was not going to allow me to die on his watch, I gave up my attempts and climbed off the chair after removing the torn t-shirt from around my neck.

The crack head who save my life then introduced himself as Bubbles and offered to let me to stay at his place for as long as I need somewhere to stay. I took him up on this offer and we became very good friends up until the time of his death caused by substance abuse. I lived with them for about four months, then I was back out on my own on the streets again, back to sleeping on that bench in Adam Smith Square. After saving my life he had me promise that I would bury him when he died and I did just that.

"Cocaine is the love taker, it takes away all the love from you" my friend Trevor Luke sang once in one of his many calypso songs. This is generally a true statement, but Hayden Gill and his lifelong partner in drugs Dexter Roberts, were no ordinary drug addicts. They had so much love and compassion in their hearts. They would share their last with you if you needed them to, no matter who you were, a bruised reed they would not break! Thank you Father God in heaven for sending them to take care of me in the time You knew I needed them. I pray that my God take into account all the good things they have done for me and have mercy on them on His day of judgment.

At twenty years old, my life went on as normal as it had come to be. I was parking cars on the side of the road at night and hiding from the taunts and teases of school children and young adults by day. It was mainly the adults living and working in my community that would frustrate me the most. The ones who see me just about each and every day and still they would stare and jeer and joke to their friends "here comes Freddie Krueger" or "look bun-up coming, run!"

Some of the most cruel and hurtful things that no human, far less a young boy, should ever have to hear was said to me. Freddie Krueger, Bun-Up, Acid, Acid Face, Predator, Bun Face, Monster, Alien, Spartan, Demon, Devil, Gorilla, De Mask, Two Face, Bun-Bun and so many more, whatever name you could think of that a tease could be associated with my face I was called. So many I would find it impossible to remember them all, but after being called by them thousands of times, they stuck in my head. Every time someone called me a hurtful name, tears would begin to build up in my eyes until one day there was finally no more tears. I was convinced within my own heart and mind that I truly had become all that they claimed that I was. Suicide was therefore still on my mind for many hours, every day.

Chapter XV

Three Strikes then Glory!

I left the capital city in 2009 and headed off to Curepe, a town about eleven miles away to the East, having had enough of the environment in the city. One night, I was digging through some trash cans in search of something to eat that would ease the hunger pain I had become quite familiar with in my stomach. I searched this one can from top to bottom but found no food. I did however come across something that cut my appetite for food and gave me an instant appetite for death once again. Buried almost to the bottom of the trash, I found a bottle filled with prescription pills. I slipped the bottle into my pants pocket, neatly fixed back the garbage that I had disrupted and disappeared into the night with a humble and pleasant smile on my face.

I was sleeping in an abandoned parking lot back then and dragged the piece of refrigerator cardboard box I slept on all the way to the back, into the dark, lonely shadows. I took it to a spot where I was convinced that no one would be able to see or hear me, no one would be able to stop me. I laid there, in the back of the parking lot on my cardboard, looking at the overcast sky and wishing for rain as my tears flowed like a gentle river of hopelessness. What is life? Why should I want to live it? Who is to say that I should not have a choice in the matter of my very own life and death? These were the questions I asked myself that early morning. Questions which, if the answers I came up with were the right ones, would have given me a reason to stop myself. Alas, none of my answers seemed right. Life was meaningless and the abundance of pain was far too much. Finally I dipped into my pocket and retrieved the bottle containing maybe about seventy pills and I swallowed them all. About two seconds after doing so, I passed out.

My eyes reopened two days later only to find myself being cared for at the Intensive Care Unit of the Eric Williams Medical Sciences Complex. God had, for the third time, saved my life from my very own hands. The only thing I could have done was to cry out to the Lord God, Creator of the heavens and the earth and that is exactly what I did. With my whole heart and soul I cried out to Him with a loud voice "God, if you are in fact real and you do in fact really exist please, I beg you, hear my cry!"

I reasoned that somehow it just might be possible that He did in fact have some sort of plan for my life. I had been trying my hardest to die but death somehow eluded me and maybe this was because He was not ready for me yet. I told God however that if He really knew all things, then He must know that more than anything else, I did not want to live this life. I did not want Romel Ravello to continue in the land of the living. I said to Him, if He would give me a reason to want to live this life, then I would live it not for myself but, I would live this life for Him!

Chapter XVI

The Glory of the Living God!

I settled down for a while after crying out to Him and something inside of me urged me to open a drawer next to my bed and investigate what was inside. There in the drawer, was a Bible placed by the Gideon's. I picked it up, held it open and started to read to myself. The gospel of John, chapter 19, was where it opened to. Within two minutes of reading, God gave me the reason I was looking for. In John 14:19, Jesus Christ was speaking to His disciples and He told them something so profound that over two thousand years later, far away in the Caribbean Seas His statement held so much power,

"Because I live, you also shall live"

I laid there in utter amazement, this word was for me! Because Jesus Christ lived I had life in Him without even considering it. He died so that I might live! I broke down into tears as I confessed my sins and my rebellion against God. I pleaded with Him for forgiveness and invited Him into my heart and life as my personal Lord and Savior. I prayed that He would teach me how to love others and more importantly, teach me how to accept my facial condition and to learn how to love myself before expecting anyone else to love me.

After praying for these things, I fell asleep for a few hours and was awoken by a nurse at around 5:15pm. She informed me that I had been discharged by the doctor and was free to go home. I got myself ready, left the hospital and headed to Curepe. I reached the car park where I tried to take my life days prior, laid down on my cardboard bed and went to sleep.

I woke up the following morning, got some breakfast and went through the day. As night came, I headed back to my car park and went to sleep. I woke up after a second restful night and went through the day cool, calm and I might even dare to say happily. It was not until about 5:00pm that afternoon that I stopped myself and pondered what it was exactly that was going on with me. I was not angry, I was not frustrated, I had not felt depressed or thought about suicide in two days. Then I realized, following my encounter with the Bible just days prior, Jesus! The Lord Jesus Christ had given me a reason to live! He had replaced my heart of stone with a soft, warm, fleshly heart in which He was dwelling!

I soon started to attend a Christian guarding called Champion Dynamics lead by Kerwin Narine and his wife Onika. Champion started off awesome, I was so on fire for God, being hungry and thirsty for His righteousness. I read His Holy Word day and night with earnest pray and offerings of praise. I worshipped Him continuously. Kerwin also allowed me to stay at a house in Woodbrook that was owned by BorderCom

International, a company in which he was part owner. Not long after, I hooked up with one of the best Christian Brothers I have met, Brook Potter.

Brook and I would spend hours on end praying for everyone we knew needed prayer. We prayed for our nation and its leaders, we prayed for the world and the various heads of governments, we prayed that God would open doors for the both of us in whatever situations we were in and we prayed for my facial reconstruction. Almost every day, Brook and I would get together to pray and worship God. He was such a good friend and brother to me, a real genuine Christian. He knew my areas of struggle and never once knocked me for them, instead he trusted that God, in starting His good work in my life, was fully well capable of completing it to His glory.

Other people at Champion Dynamics on the other hand did not hold the same view as Brook did. After they started to join our prayer sessions the group grew from two to five, ten to twenty. I had a friend set up an altar on the back of his truck from where I preached about God's love and the availability of forgiveness of sins to anyone who called on the Christ Jesus. However, I was told by the others that I could not preach the gospel if I was still smoking cigarettes and marijuana, so they enlisted me into a rehabilitation center.

I gave it my best try but ran away from there at the start of the third day when they told me that I was not allowed to read the bible while I was there. I did not understand why they had this rule and concluded that this place just was not for me. They enrolled me into yet another rehab facility which I stay in one week before I stormed out after being asked to program their computer for them free of charge. Work for free, no way, no thank you, good bye!

Champion Dynamics wanted nothing to do with me after this so I went on my own way, I was once again however homeless, back to sleeping in Adam Smith Square and the Phase II Pan Yard.

Chapter XVII

The Prime Minister and I

In June of 2009 I decided to make an attempt to see then Prime Minister, and my childhood friend, Mr. Patrick Manning. I had not gone to see him since I got the triangle card from him to Minister Yuille-Williams so that she could have equipped me fully for Islamic school in 2002. He had not seen me with the burn on my face nor had I ever brought to his attention the extremeness of my living conditions.

Mr. Manning would always see members of the public at his constituency office in San Fernando East every Thursday afternoon as long as he was on the island. However, one would normally need to book an appointment in most cases months in advance, to get the opportunity to express your concerns to the Prime Minister. On Thursday morning, Jason Williams gave me a very nice black fitted dress suit and I got to Mr. Manning's office at around 1:00pm. I asked the receptionist if it was possible for me to have a few minutes of Mr. Manning's time despite not having an appointment. No matter how hard they tried to turn me away, I was not persuaded to leave. They told me no because there were well over seventy people already there with appointments as well as others who did not have appointments but had too big of a social status to be turned away and also members of the local media wanting the Prime Minister's time to address their questions.

Mr. Manning himself had not yet arrived so I decided to wait in the stairway hoping by some miracle that I would be able to stop him on his way in and talk to him. He arrived at around 2:10pm and was swarmed by a barrage of people. His security had to encircle him to prevent people from pulling and tugging on him with their loving embrace of hugs and kisses. I did not even come close to having a chance for our eyes to even connect, far less me being able to say a single word to him. Nevertheless, I was not ready to give up. I stood out in the hallway in the full view of the staff for hours until about 10:30pm. With the majority of persons waiting to see Mr. Manning having left by then, I stepped back into the office and again asked if they would be so kind as to allow me to speak to the Prime Minister for just a few minutes. I indicated that I would be willing to wait until I was the very last person so as to not offend anyone who had made a booking prior to the day. Karlene, his personal assistant told me to have a seat and she would try to see what she could do.

At 10:49pm Karleen called me to meet with Mr. Manning. I took a deep breath and walked with her into his office. Mr. Manning greeted me and asked me what my name was as he shook my hand and motioned that I could have a seat. "Romel Ravello, Honourable Prime Minister" was my reply. We both sat down and he proceeded to write my name down as he did for everyone who came to visit him. As he wrote down my name he repeated it to himself, then again under his breath, as if he were pondering as to whether he had heard the name before. Suddenly he stopped and began to look up at me. As he looked up raising his right index finger, he pointed at me with a look of confusion on his face, "Romel Ravello?" he asked. "Yes Prime Minister, I am that little boy who used to come see you every Monday afternoon back when you were the Leader of the Opposition."

He flew up out of his chair with the most genuine look of care and concern on his face, with both his arms outstretched wide. "Romel is it really you? What happened? Why I was not made aware of this? Why had you not come to me much sooner?" were some of the questions he asked as he quickly made his way across the desk and embraced me like a long lost friend. We sat and talked for a lengthy period of time after this. He even had his staff serve me dinner as well. We discussed all that I had been through during the time since we last connected and he expressed to me that he was sorry that he had not known what I was going through. He assured me that he would do everything in his power to assist me towards my all round development.

The Prime Minister proceeded to call the Minister of Health, who had just landed at the airport returning from a health summit somewhere in the world. He told him that he would be sending me to see him the next morning and he gave Minister Narace the green light for him and the Ministry to take measures above and beyond normal, to do everything that could be done to assist my case. He went further to state that he would proceed as far as even bringing my case before Cabinet to discuss and agree on measure that could be taken regardless of the price.

We sat down for about an hour more afterwards, discussing all manner of things and planning what direction my life should take from that point onwards because according to the Prime Minister "God had a hand in all of this". He firmly believed that God had connected us years earlier for His divine plan and purpose. He confided in me that he had a spiritual advisor and that he would like the opportunity to introduce me to her if that was okay with me. I agreed to such. "Romel, when she speaks it is not her that is speaking, rather it is actually God that is speaking through her!" I looked at him puzzled, "Can your mind comprehend what I am saying to you Romel? When she opens her mouth and speaks it is not she that is speaking, but the Creator God, speaking through her!". "Yes, I understand what you are saying to me Honorable Prime Minister, I would love to meet her" I said to him, shaken and disturbed in my spirit. Was this for real?

Did the Prime Minister of my country have direct access to the Throne Room of Heaven, the ear of the Lord God Almighty at his disposal? What a mighty man he is if this was indeed so, but my mind found it hard to conceive the notion of God the Father actually speaking. What would his voice sound like I wondered.

As soon as I got back to Woodbrook I called Brook Potter and asked his opinion on the matter. After filling him in on the details given to me by the Prime Minister, he then told me of some of the things that he had heard from other people, but not from anyone that could have actually proved to have met the woman. He also told me about a video in which televangelist Benny Hinn had spoken ill of the same woman and referred to Prime Minister Manning as a "foolish man" for believing in that woman.

Brook however concluded that he had no opinion on the woman and that he was rather envious of me for having the opportunity to meet her. "I wish I could meet Reverend Juliana Pena!" he exclaimed. There, on that very night I purposed in my heart that I wanted to find out for myself whether or not the Creator God was in fact speaking through Juliana Pena, as Mr. Manning had so confidently tried to assure me.

I outlined the test that I was about to give her in exact detail to Brook and some other friends. On Tuesday, I got to the Prime Minister's St. Clair office and met with him and Reverend Pena. Without going into exact details, I will say that the Reverend failed my test and it really did not surprise me. Afterwards, I told this to Brook and it did not surprise him either.

Over the course of the next two months, I still spent many days with her and the more time I spent with her, the more I was certain she was not the person that my Prime Minister, with all honesty in his heart, portrayed her to be. However, I kept up the act because Mr. Manning had the government working on securing my visa to go to the United States to have my facial surgeries and I selfishly did not want to interrupt that process. This is the guilt that I have carried in my heart for the past few years.

One day after spending time with Reverend Pena at her Maraval residence, she surprisingly showed me the video that was posted on YouTube where Benny Hinn was speaking about her and the Prime Minister. I said nothing when she showed it to me, but after watching it with her, I was encouraged to see someone of Benny Hinn's stature speaking about her in the same way in which I thought of her. This gave me the testicular fortitude to approach the Prime Minister about the subject matter. I went home that night and rehearsed exactly what I was going to say to him the following day.

I planned to say to Mr. Manning, 'Prime Minister please forgive me, but I have been lying to you about Ms. Pena the whole time. The five different things I related to her never happened. I made them all up. I did it because I was a little bit concerned when you told me that it was "God speaking through her" so I wanted to be sure that it really was God. Now Honorable Prime Minister I am not trying to say that she is a fake, but simply that I was fake, and in light of her confirming or rather "God" confirming the things and stating them to be true, I humbly request that you look into the matter and perhaps test it for yourself. If something is a lie then God will never claim it to be the truth because God cannot lie.'

Instead of manning up and telling the truth to Mr. Manning however, I folded and cowardly kept my mouth shut. It happened that the minute the Prime Minister opened the door and shook my hand. Without me prompting the subject, he said to me "Romel, I hope you can understand that I will never allow people like Benny Hinn back into my presence. He can't even step into my office. What do you want to talk to me about?" This statement, being so out of the blue caused me to chicken out. I told him it was nothing and I was just stopping by to thank him once again for assistance with my visa and my reconstructive surgery.

Chapter XVIII

The Windy City

Finally on October 13th 2009, I was in the United States of America for the very first time, heading to Chicago to have surgery performed by Dr. Jay Pensler at Northwestern Memorial Hospital in downtown Chicago. But by this time I was so spiritually confused and messed up by all of the whirlwind of events that took place over the course of the year that I was just about ready to give up on God again. I just needed one more mishap within the church to push me away from God.

I got to Chicago and it was wonderful! The buildings were so tall, the city so big. It was nothing short of stunning, but the most stunning part of it all was when I walked through the streets of America I was just a normal, everyday guy walking along the sidewalk like everyone else! No one was staring at me, no one was laughing, little children were not making fun of me or drawing attention to the scars on my face. It was utterly amazing! I was free. Free to go into any store I wanted to go into, free to eat at which ever restaurant I choose to eat at, free to hop into a cab without being told by the driver to get out, free to ride the bus or train without other passengers wanting to getting off. I was the happiest guy in the world.

One evening I attended a service at a church in Chicago's downtown area where I spoke with a few pastors who invited me to tell the congregation a little bit about my trip. While dining at the church in downtown one Sunday afternoon I was introduced to a woman by one of the pastors. We exchanged numbers and she began calling me. We would talk about all manner of things until one day she confessed that she had very strong feelings towards me and not long after meeting, myself and this much older lady, whom I met in church, were engaging in activities that were sexually immoral.

In January 2010 when it was time for me to go home, she caused such a ruction for me between both the downtown and south side churches that by the time my plane landed in Trinidad, I had considered myself no long a believer in God but rather that I was now Anti-Theist. The culmination of my third suicide attempt, giving my life to Christ and feeling rejected by the local churches, my meetings with Reverend Pena, the web I got myself into with the churches in Chicago and not ultimately finding what I was looking in terms of my relationship with God, led to my new revelation. At best I considered myself to be Existentialist, the complete opposite to being a Christian and I sorted out to achieve my very own righteousness.

I have to admit that this worked out pretty well for my outer being. I had evolved into to an ultra-kind, caring, giving, humble, respectful, polite and mannerly person, knowing that my attitude had to be better than the attitudes of those who professed to be Christians, but in no way walked like Christ. I strived to prove that even with the absence of God from my life that I could still be a better person than most of them.

Chapter XIX

Save Ah Spot Fuh Meh Nah

With my new outlook on life, things were going great for me in Trinidad. My roadside car park hustle was turning into something of an official business which was known as "Save Ah Spot Fuh Meh Nah". I had call cards for persons to contact me to let me know when they would be coming to the club to reserve their parking spot. I had phone numbers, Blackberry Messenger pin numbers, Facebook, Twitter and email addresses to reach me. Parking was TT$100 per spot and business was booming.

I was making an average of TT $10,000-$12,000 per month as all of the rich and famous people on the island who partied at 51 Degrees, parked their vehicles with Save Ah Spot Fuh Meh Nah. I had VIP Roadside parking just outside the front door of the club and no matter what hour of the night you came, you could have been sure that Romel had a VIP parking spot for you.

After running my business for about two years, I got a phone call from business guru and one of the main shareholders at 51 Degrees, Victor Sooknarine. He told me that he was on his way to pick me up so that we could discuss some business. Months earlier I had asked him for a loan to invest in earthquake alarms, which he had initially found to be foolish. He picked me up and we headed off to Movie Towne where we discussed in detail my earthquake alarm plan. After which, he made an unbelievable deal with me, one that was by far one of the greatest offers I had ever gotten. We agreed that I would be the Assistant Manager of Cariflex (1994) Limited, one of the companies he inherited following the death of his father Harry Sooknarine a year prior. The deal made was that I would work there for three months and if I could prove to him that I was capable of conducting the operations of the everyday running of a company, then he would give me the US$25,000.00 needed to start up my own company, giving it to me as a gift and not a loan. My ego soared! It seemed as if Existentialism was working out pretty well for me. I was making a lot of money, making new friends, doing something that I really enjoyed and now I was the Assistant Manager of one of the largest printing companies in the Caribbean!

Working at Cariflex was not what I expected, I did not have much to do, however it was a great learning experience and it was awesome. Every evening I had the opportunity to ride with and talk to one of the biggest "big boys" of the island Victor Sooknarine. He would drop me off at Cipriani Boulevard, where I was living in a nearby abandoned house. I chose to live there having settled into that kind of lifestyle and it provided me with a place to stay that was rent free. Weeks turned into months and before I knew it I was working there for over a year and loving it. The deal we initially made was never realized or discussed. I was also still parking cars on the weekend as I also had Fridays off from Cariflex. Victor also paid for me to get back into law school, following my stint at the University of the West Indies for one month back in 2008. He gave me everything I asked him for, laptop, smartphones, money, clothes, trips abroad, V.I.P. tickets to parties, island get-away vacation for my birthday, and he even allowed me to live in the company's million dollar house and much more. One day he even allowed me to wear his US$20,000.00 Rolex Daytona.

Victor was not much a good boss to work for. He would yell at you and curse you out for the slightest little thing, but around five o'clock when it was time to go home, he would once again be my really good friend who I could talk to about anything as we cruised down the highway in his S600 Mercedes Benz.

One night as I was lying on my bed in the house that Victor had provided for me, the voice of the Lord spoke to me.

"Romel, Victor Sooknarine is trying to plan out your life. He does not know that I killed Mark Guerra for that same thing."

What? The statement in my head came as a complete shock to me. Nevertheless, it was God. It was God saying to me that He had directly intervened, even to the point as to end someone's life, so that His ultimate plan for me would not fail and it seemed as if he was telling me that He would do whatever it took for Victor's plan to come to naught.

I had been holding on to a cheque that Victor had given me to pay for my exams for weeks and the very next morning I gave the check back to him. I told him that I was not yet ready to write my law exams to go on to become one of his personal lawyers. He was disappointed but simply claimed to have understood. I told him nothing about the dream. He promised to give me an increase in salary for my good work, but within three weeks of hearing about what had been done to Mark Guerra on my account, Victor was laying on a bed in the ICU of the St. Clair Private Hospital after crashing his S600 Benz. One person died and two others were severely injured in this accident. Two weeks later I quit my job as Assistant Manager, never fully explaining to Victor why I left, who was still at the time on bed rest. I moved back to Woodbrook and continued parking cars. Victor never did give me the $25,000 of investment money, but he taught me a lot about business, about people and also about myself.

I have come to realize that back then I was only looking at the outside condition of Christians, both in my native island and abroad. The human fleshy side, so much so that I had neglected to look at my own inward condition of my soul. On the inside, I continued growing to be mean, nasty, angry, violent and an altogether miserable person. My life was once again meaningless. This time however, my meaninglessness did not come as a result of the abundance of pain. On the contrary, meaninglessness came about as a result of the abundance of pleasure. I would further come to realize that this meaninglessness also came from the absence of God and that rejecting God had rendered my life meaningless.

I was enjoying the finer things in life once more, I was making money, I was connected to some of the richest super-elites that my country had to offer, there were even a few girls admitting to liking me, yet I was still so empty inside. Emptiness that I tried everything I could on my own to fill. I had purchased a few other friends who had come to believe in my abilities and together we even formed our very own political party. The People's Servants Political Party came into being after I felt abandoned by the political party that I belonged to, the UNC, following their change of leadership, Being the most charismatic and dynamic speaker of the group of youths, I became the Political Leader and we were working on our plans and manifesto to contest the 2015 general election.

On one side of the spectrum, life was awesome. I had everything I felt like I wanted. Save Ah Spot Fuh Meh Nah was earning me an average revenue of TT$12,000.00 every month. Amalfi Distributors, another company I launched, was also about to be awarded a few marketing and distribution contracts because of a few connections that I still held within the present governmental regime from back in the Basdeo Panday era. My political ambition was also slowly starting to show fruit as a few prominent citizens started to communicate with my party, The People's

Servants Political Servant dealt mainly with our intentions to have marijuana de-criminalized in Trinidad and Tobago.

Carnival 2013 had just ended and I was feeling as if I was on top of the world. I partied from Mai Tai to Last-lap enjoying to the fullest the moral debridement of my country just like almost every other Trinidadian, what a sad state of affairs indeed.

Chapter XX

Back to the Windy City Again

Immediately following Carnival, I had to fly to Chicago to see Dr. Pensler again because I had an infectious area developing on the right side of my face that needed medical attention. The government had covered all aspects of my expenditure. I headed to the Piarco International Airport on February 16th to catch my 9:00am American Airlines flight. I was scheduled to fly from Trinidad to Houston, Texas where I had a connecting flight which would have had me landing at the O'Hare International Airport in Chicago at around 6:15pm.

At 8:04am, I approached the hostess at the American Airlines ticketing counter and produced my passport and flight confirmation number. "I'm sorry Mr. Ravello, you're a bit too late. We are no longer issuing boarding passes for that flight, boarding has already commenced." She went on to inform me that the most that could be done would be to put me on stand-by for a flight the following day but American Airlines could not guaranteed that there would in fact be a seat available for me. I was advised that the best option I had was to purchase the very last available seat for that said flight in the Business Class cabin at an additional US$700.00. After pleading with her throughout the time she was telling me all of this, I finally realized that there was absolutely no way that this lady was going to issue me my boarding pass so that I could even attempt to clear security and immigration officials in time.

All of a sudden, I completely lost my mind and starting flipping out on her. In an instant I was hooting and hollering, attacking her with a barrage of insults. I told her everything from how ugly she was to exactly how her mother made her. I yelled every curse word known to man at her as I stomped my feet and crazily flung my arms in the air. Despite the fact that I was carrying on in such an extremely rude, disrespectful and aggressive manner, she did not allow my unwarranted behavior to breakdown her level of professionalism. She remained calm, respectful and polite throughout my malicious verbal attack. This got me even more riled up given the fact that she was able to go on with business as normal, when I was not allow to board my flight. This was the main thing that provoked my anger to the next level.

Out of the depths of my empty, fragile, hopeless, depressed, frustrated, and selfishly foolish heart, came the by far biggest mistake I had ever made in my short, sorrowful and miserable life. My emotions erupted and I went off! "If I ever see you in the streets you're a dead woman" I sternly said while looking her dead in the eye. "If I ever find out where you live, I will kill your entire family, your parents, your husband, your children, even your pets!" Well, my threats got their desired effect and the airline representative picked up the little white phone and made a short call.

The island of Trinidad is a relatively small island with a population of around one million nationals. It would take you just about three hours to drive from opposite ends. Everyone basically knows everyone somehow or the other, and if you don't know a person directly or indirectly, it is not hard to find out whatever you need to know about any person through some connection.

It would take a guy like me no more than one week to find out who you are, what your name is, where you live, who you bank with, the number of vehicles you drove, their license plate numbers and anything else I wanted to know about you. I was good at this because in the VIP car parking service, it paid big bucks to know who was who and to be aware of the type of business they did. Conversations and opportunities became a lot easier when you had prior knowledge of the person you were trying to convince to pay five times the price for a parking spot that really should be free! Yup I knew all about finding out about people.

I learned firsthand from my actions at the airport however, that you definitely cannot make any type of treat in an international airport since September 11th 2001. Within two minutes of her hanging up that little white phone, there were four police officers of the Piarco International Airport Drug Trafficking and Terrorism Branch all over me.

I was detained and taken away to a special integration room where I was questioned and then informed that American Airlines was filing the paper work to have me blacklisted.

The shame and guilt of my actions consumed me. When the officers explained to me the ramifications of being blacklisted, that I would never again be allowed to fly on any airline from any airport in any part of the world, it was honestly the least of my worries. I was by far most concerned about the direction my life was heading. I was by far more consumed with the thought of how I foolishly and selfishly debunked the very notion of God's existence, had daily mocked His Holy name and waged war against anyone that tried to persuade me towards His direction.

It seemed as though the more I rejected God, the angrier at life I became. Suicide was no longer on my mind, but my heart had once again become bitter towards my fellow men and my life. Even though on the surface my life seemed to be going well, it was completely hollow and meaningless once again. This time however, I was in a far worst state than ever before. Despite all of the things He had done for me, I allowed myself to get so far off track that it felt good to deny Him. You see that's what it all really boiled down to, me wanting to feel good.

After I returned from Chicago the first time in 2010, Carnival was right around the corner and I had so many mixed and different opinions about who God really was and in wanting to do my own thing such as enjoy the national festival without the remorse of spiritual guilt in my heart. I found it a lot easier to say that God was dead and did not exist than to abstain from the lustful desires of the fleshly canal heart. It felt like such a relief to say to myself that there was no universal moral law-giver and therefore there could not be a universal moral law. But in convincing myself of this, I erased the line that separated the things that are morally right from the things that were morally wrong which were ultimately set by God.

I attempted to replace these things with my very own definition of what was right and wrong. For you see, without a defined line, it is so easy to mix the two up without even knowing it and I was about to pay for blurring the difference. I was about to be permanently grounded, my wings were about to be clipped.

In a loud sorrowful voice to the shock of the officers in the room and even to my own utter amazement, my mouth opened and I could do nothing but cry aloud onto the Lord. I cried out not for help in my situation but rather I cried out for help for my troubled soul. "Look at this person I have become Lord, in all of my pain and suffering I did not become as angry of a soul as I am now." I contended with God "I don't deserve to live, I have not stopped cursing Your name, day and night my mouth has spoken ill of you and now look at trouble my mouth continues to put me in." With tears, mucus and saliva soaking my shirt, I cried out to him in a loud voice until I threw up.

"Romel, why do you war against My will over your life so much?"

A powerful, beautiful and authoritative voice suddenly asked my spirit interrupting my outburst. "Is that you Lord? Is it really you?" I questioned. The officers in the room all came closer and paid pin-drop attention to what was being said. They realized that I had entered into dialect with the Lord God Almighty. No one dared to interrupt nor did any opt to leave the room.

"I am the Lord God, I am your Father. I have brought you into existence and I and I alone have sustained you from your childhood. Never one day have I left you. I was always with you and always had My hand on your life. When you were a small boy, I proclaimed that you would be set aside for My chosen purpose and from since then your enemy has tried and tried to destroy your life but I have not allowed it! Why do you try so hard to fight against My will? Don't you know that I am the One who appoints the role that every man should play in this life and that I was the One who appointed yours? Why won't you yield to My will Romel? I know the plans I have for you and no matter how much you fight it, My plan will come to reality. Why don't you walk with Me Romel? Why don't you allow me to empty you out and fill you the way I want you to be filled? I want

you to be filled with happiness and joy. I want to bless you beyond measure for I have a great work for you to do for My glory's sake."

"Could you use me Lord? I have been such a rebel towards Your word and Your Name. It's not possible for you to use me" I replied

"I am God! I can use whoever, whatever and whenever. I used Saul and made him into the great apostle Paul. I will use you also, you only need to completely trust Me. Lay everything in your heart at the cross now and do whatever I tell you to do and go where ever I tell you to go and I will use you."

"I will do whatever you tell me to do and go where ever you tell me to go Lord. I will be Your servant, use me".

"When you get to Chicago this afternoon I will tell you what to do"

I became puzzled when He told me this as the papers were presently being filed for me to be blacklisted.

"Why worry about what I told you? Know that I am God and rejoice for I will deliver you from this trouble just as I have done so many times in the past and today when you land in Chicago, you will know that I the Lord your God, am able to do all things rejoice"

"God if you are able to deliver me out of this mess, then I swear that whatever I do with my life, I will bring glory and honor onto Your Holy name."

The conversation lasted for a about fifteen minutes while the officers looked on. I took the council of the Lord and I began to sing out aloud a song of praise that popped into my head

> *...Hallelujah thank you Jesus, Lord Your worthy*
> *of all the glory and all the honor and all the praise*
> *It makes me want to shout Hallelujah, thank you Jesus...*

I was able to rejoice and praise the Lord to the amazement of those surrounding me because the Spirit of the Lord caused His peace to rest on me and I found it to be true that His peace surpasses all understanding. I did not fully understand what I was rejoicing about, but it did not take more than five seconds for me to find out.

Before I could have finished singing the chorus to the song, the General Manager of American Airlines Operations rushed through the doors to the interrogation room. "Officers we don't need you anymore" he exclaimed "We are no longer filing to have Mr. Ravello blacklisted!" He went on to explain that he read up on my story and that he would do everything in his power to have me at my doctor's appointment on time.

He informed me that they were working on putting me on a flight bound for Miami, then have me connect to another flight to Chicago and I would be there by 10:10pm tonight. He also gave me his name and telephone number and told me that if I ever again need any help regarding flights to and from my doctors, that I should feel free to give him a call! So it happened, just as the Lord said it would, I was in Chicago that very night.

That is exactly what happened! I am sure the police officers in that room that day would be happy to testify about its truth. I held a long, loud verbal conversation with the Savior and Redeemer of my soul. He once again after so many times gone by, proved Himself to be a mighty, powerful and awesome God, capable of opening doors that no man could ever shut and shutting those that are unable to again be opened by human hands. He is able, our God is able, to do exceedingly and abundantly far above all things our human minds could ever think of or imagine.

Chapter XXI

Reflections from Above

As the plane took off from the ground at the Piarco International Airport, I looked out my cabin window and saw my native island once again shrink in size as the pilot climbed to his cruising altitude. He leveled out at about 40,000 feet in the air and I looked down at the clouds and at the ocean. A view I should have never again have had the opportunity to see, had God not directly intervened. I threw my seat back, pulled my blanket and closed the window shade.

I thanked God again as I started to reflect on my life, on the things written in this book and so much more. I reflected on how great and merciful God was to me, I reflected on the cross, on my sinful past. I remembered the troubles and hardships of my childhood. I remembered the pain and suffering of my youth. I reflected how God had been my comfort even when I did not know it. I remember most of all of His promises over my life and my promise made to Him as He delivered me in the time of my deepest trouble. My eyes closed as my mind journeyed on everything that lead up to this point.

I sat on that plane reflecting on the fact that by the time I was fifteen years old, I had already been remanded twice and convicted once, all at the adult jail, all for the most minor of offensives like loitering.

Then I reflected on September 2004, when that person threw acid on my face as I slept on that bench. I reflected on how by the Spring of 2009, at the age of twenty I had already attempted suicide three times, all, evidently to no avail. Then October of that same year I travelled to the United States of America, the first of six trips thus far.

I reflected on my belief that had I been maybe the only man who could have been convincing enough to have perhaps made former Prime Minister Manning think twice about calling an early general election in 2010. I was indeed in a position as a personal friend to tell Mr. Manning that his spiritual advisor was misadvising him. But I failed to speak to him that day at his St. Clair office and it's a regret I still live with.

I reflected on how foolishly I had in 2012 once again abandoned the notion of a Creator God. Being so foolishly blinded, I claimed to be good without God, boasting of my great accomplishments of being "over my face", and ascending myself up to the assistant managerial position at Cariflex. My fame was growing but not as big as my ego. I was capable of talking my way into any deal, or, out of any scenario. I had infiltrated the upper class circle in the most simplest of ways and felt as though I was some sort of undercover king. That I was the greatest "nobody" my country had ever produced. Maybe I was just the biggest fool at the time for not recognizing what was God's grace over my troubled soul.

Finally I reflected on the present day as I sat comfortably 40,000 feet in the air. It was the 16th day of February, the day I was scheduled to fly to Chicago at 9:00am via American Airlines. A flight I was not able to make it to, but yet here I was sitting on a plane, the day that God, with a Mighty Hand, revealed Himself to me. He saved me and changed the course of my life forever.

"I am God! When you get to Chicago this afternoon I will tell you what to do!"

To me it still seemed beyond impossible that I could be in Chicago this day. My situation seemed like certain doom, but the Blood of the Lamb spoke better things, so I decided in my heart to believe the report of the Lord.

I got to Miami and connected to another American Airlines flight to Chicago. God's words were indeed true and when I got to Chicago He indeed told me what to do. He spoke to me at the Signature Restaurant and Bar in the John Hancock Tower. He reminded me of all the childhood dreams, memories and ambitions I had. He told me to write about my life so that He could show me, and even the world, how He has always been near to the poor and brokenhearted like me. He told me that it was time for His word over my life to bear fruit, that I would stand before great multitudes and proclaim the gospel of His love and mercy and grace. That I would reassure hearts and convince minds that He still saves, and that He still is capable of doing exceedingly and abundantly far more than we could ever ask for or think of. That He is still yet able to rescue both man and his soul and give to us life. He told me that through my life story this would be done.

Chapter XXII

A Friend for the Road

When the Lord God started to map out the journey for me, I became afraid. I asked God to have someone else go with me so that I might not have to stand alone. In some ways I really wanted a friend along the way, but God knows the heart of every man. The Lord knew that I was really putting the name of Jesus Christ to the test. Like Abraham I felt myself saying 'seeing that I have been bold enough to speak to the One who formed me from the dust', I requested of Him that Jameel Roberts accompany me on my mission. Even Jameel knew that there was no way in this world for him to get a U.S. Visa and if it were to happen, it would surely be an act of divine grace.

The Lord said to me,

"return to Trinidad get Jameel and return to Chicago on April 20th 2013"

So, the next day, with surgery having been rescheduled through the intervention of God, I got on a plane and headed back to Trinidad to tell Jameel and my brother Randy everything that happened and to prepare Jameel. He laughed for the first four weeks, but when he saw April 20th approaching, he started to take heart a little. I did manage to get him to send in his application and go to the interview and every day I would encourage him and aggravate him at the same time. "Jameel in twenty days we're going to be in America" I would say to him. "Romel I do not have a U.S. visa" he would reply.

One local news station, CNC3, aired a story about the surgery I was about to do and this resulted in many citizens contributing to the non-surgical expenses to help my case. The business sector also provided their assistance, for which I am ever grateful to companies such as Super Industrial Services (SIS) Limited, Premier Customs Brokers Limited and The National Gas Company.

I continued telling Jameel, "Jameel, in ten days we're going to America!" "Romel, I don't have a US visa!" was Jameel's reply again. Meanwhile I was busy carrying on with other areas of my life, meeting with people like Harry Boodoosingh, DJ Hyper Hopper, Jason 'JW' Williams and my good friend Jules Sobion.

"Jameel, in five days we are going to America, make sure you take your time and pack your bags properly and plan exactly what things you want to carry because it's going to be a long trip" I texted to him. He called me so that I would again hear him say that he does not have a visa, nor does he qualify to get a visa, the embassy was not going to give him a visa and that we had wasted the money we spent on his application. Still, on April 18th I called him to reassure him that in just two days we would be gone, for it was the date that the Lord had appointed me to return to Chicago. Jameel was almost furious, he told me that he was not having that conversation with me again and hung up the phone.

On April 19th at about 2:10pm, I got an ecstatic phone call from Jameel as he yelled "Romel! The U.S. Embassy just called me and told me to go pick up my passport containing my visa at DHL's head office! Romel, tomorrow we're going to America, you're going to write that book and you going to start your mission!"

There we stood, Jameel and I in the parking lot of the Ft. Lauderdale International Airport en route to Chicago on April 20th 2013, the very day God appointed back in February. The execution of the Lord's plan He gave me for acquiring Jameel's visa was flawless. The systems He put in place and the people The Lord put to administer them was nothing short of divine. It was at that time I asked the question "What are you going to do with your life Romel Ravello? The world wants you to do law, do economics, business management or maybe politics". I reflected on the Lord and all He had done for me. I knew there was something greater that He had called me to or maybe I didn't understand the power of my testimony and how able it is to defeat the enemy when it's washed in the power of the blood of the Lamb.

I decided to wait on the Lord to point the direction of my life, but I had no intentions of waiting still. My original plan was to go to Chicago, see Dr. Jay Pensler my plastic surgeon, and then have Jameel and I make our way to Cincinnati, Ohio to visit a friend of mine so that I could sit down and pen the story of my life as the Lord instructed me to. Not only that, I also purposed in my heart to start sharing my life story testimony to encourage others to realize what God is capable of doing in their lives; if they simply believed His promises. By reporting to the saints the great things He's done in my life, many have since reaffirmed their faith in His ability.

Jameel however was able to convince me to have us travel to Buffalo, New York to his uncle's house instead, citing that there I would have all the comforts I needed to allow me to be able to relax and write my book, as well as the fact that there were many great churches in Buffalo to visit. We flew to Chicago that night and with surgery postponed again, the following night flew into Buffalo. The first morning in New York, I headed off to Barnes and Noble bookstore to purchase a Bible. We then went to Best Buy and purchased a laptop computer and all the things I would need to write my story.

It was in Buffalo, in the summer of 2013 that I got baptized at Renovation Church. It was also there that I met my now very good friend and sister Janice Miller, who has been an excellent prayer partner and a great ear to listen to me when I needed someone. I eventually ran out of money and accommodation in New York having exhausted my time at Jameel's relatives' home. Things got so bad that I had to take my laptop, with the incomplete manuscript on it to a pawn shop in New York. I pawned it for $150 before jumping onto a bus heading to Cincinnati, Ohio. Jameel remained in Buffalo.

God had been extremely gracious to me while I was in New York. My friends that I made on previous trips to the states welcomed me warmly and made me feel like an honored guest from the minute I walked into the door until I left. I was never used to that kind of love. Another love I learned to develop in New York was for my brothers and my family. I had some Puerto Rican friends that I would hang out with every day in Buffalo who introduced me to a kind of love I have never experienced. I never witnessed as much love from a family as the one they had for each other. They weren't a perfect family, to the contrary, they were highly dysfunctional with endless problem between themselves, but boy did they still love each other. They allowed nothing to come between or before that unconditional love for each other.

My friend Ian Marcum, had about eight months earlier told me via Facebook that he had moved out of his parent's house and had his own apartment in Ohio. He expressed a desire for me to come visit him, assuring me that I was most welcome to stay with him at any time. It was for this reason that I had intended to go to Ohio in the first place. By the time I got there that August morning, I had just two dollars in my pocket, one pair of jeans and two shirts in my bag, along with my Bible, a blanket and a pillow. I had a further 25 miles to go to get to Hamilton, Ohio where Ian lived. I decided to call him to ask if he could have organized a ride to come pick me up about an hour's drive from his apartment. I changed one of the dollars into four quarters, found a phone booth and dialed Ian's number. His phone was out of service. I tried calling it for nearly an hour with the same result until the pay phone somehow stole my fifty cents. I was reduced to $1.50. "I know where he lives! I know his address!" I declared to myself. "I'll walk" I concluded and started walking.

It was about 7:00am when I first started off. I walked and I walked and then I continued to walk some more. By lunchtime I started praying as I walked and stuck my thumb out in an attempt to hitch a ride while I kept walking. At about two in the afternoon I looked back and saw a white BMW 3 series coming towards me that was seemingly slowing down as I attempted to stop him. The car slowed as it passed me, then sped up. I continued walking as the BMW disappeared ahead of me.

At this very moment, the Spirit of the Lord questioned a guy named Scott Rimer as he drove home talking to God about the direction his life was heading and asking God to just show him His glory. The Holy Spirit asked Scott what he was really looking for. Was he looking for what he wanted to see, or what it is the Lord was willing to show him? He confessed to the Spirit that he wanted to see that which God was doing. He inquired of the Lord of what he should do and the Spirit said to him,

"turn around, go back and pick him up."

As I continued walking, I saw what looked like the same BMW coming back towards my direction on the opposite side of road. It turned at the intersection ahead of me and stopped. I quickly walked towards the car, with what felt like the absolute last bit of energy in my body. "Where are you going?" The driver of the white BMW asked me. Gasping for a breath to talk after walking so many hours in the hot Ohio summer weather, I finally said "If you could give me a lift to Route 4, from there I could get to my buddy's house in Hamilton, I would be very grateful. Or, however far would be fine". With a bewildered look on his face he replied "Okay hop in, but no funny stuff!" "Sir, the most dangerous thing I have on me is my Bible" I quipped back at him. He chuckled and introduced himself as Scott Rimer.

We made quick conversation both understanding that God was indeed at work in us meeting, Scott was a writer, businessman, father, husband and many other things but most of all he was a humble soul. Willing and listening for when God would use him for His glory. Waiting for an experience to point the direction in which his life should go. It didn't take long for him to offer to take me all the way to Hamilton to Ian's apartment, "what's his address?" he asked me "#8 West Victory

Drive Hamilton, Ohio. 45013." I told him as he punched it into the GPS of his iPhone. "That address is not valid" Scott informed me. I was puzzled, I was certain that this was the address Ian gave to me eight months prior and I had reviewed it many times. I knew exactly what it looked like. I even knew what the street and buildings around looked like as well thanks to Google Earth. I knew the horseshoe shaped street that was Victory Drive. I knew what the elementary school behind the apartment building looked like. I knew that it was the fourth building from the corner, it had to be valid! "Try it again, I know it's correct, 8 West Victory Drive, Hamilton, Ohio. 45013." "Same thing buddy, no results found" Scott told me once again.

After wondering for a minute or two, I informed Scott that I knew where Ian's mother lived, having previously visited Ian at this address in the spring of 2010. I asked Scott if he would take me there as I was certain that I would be able to get to Ian's apartment from there. I gave him the address and his GPS locked on. Finally, we made our way to the house of Mrs. Patti Page, Ian's mother. We got there at about three in the afternoon and I called out at the gate of the family's Greenwood Avenue address. Ms. Patti came outside, one hand raised to her eyes shading them from the reflection of the sun. "Hi Ms. Patti. I'm Ian's friend, Romel from Trinidad." She remembered me of course from my 2010 visit when I was there to see a friend from Trinidad who lived there at that time. This was back when I first met Ian and we became friends.

I told Ms. Patti and her husband Ronny about the issue we were having in finding Ian's address on the GPS. She confirmed that the address was accurate, then she informed me that I was unable to reach her son on his cell phone because Ian was in jail. "He's been there for the past three weeks" she told us. They went on to tell that Ian was hanging out and drinking with the wrong crowd, got drunk, broke into a house and stole a bunch of stuff from inside. Ian, being so drunk, didn't even make it into the house. He passed out on the front lawn and when the police came they found him still asleep at the scene of the crime, but the items were somehow recovered at his apartment. His friends went into hiding and Ian took the fall for the felony.

Ms. Patti and Ronny also explained to me that they had no room for me to stay at their home as Ian's sister was there with her three kids and one on the way. There was also Devin, Ms. Patti's other son and Jacob, Ronny's son. The house was completely full and they were not sure how to help me and had no idea where the keys for Ian's apartment were. Here I was, in the middle of Ohio with $1.50 in my pocket and I didn't know anyone else in the entire mid-west. I was devastated.

Scott began telling me not to worry and that God would work something out for me. He told me that we would go to the local YMCA and explain the whole situation to them and maybe they would be able to help. So we headed off to the YMCA. When we got there we spoke to the two ladies at the front desk who explained to us that there were no systems in place to assist someone in my position as I did not have a social security number. Scott called a few other organizations and all of them responded with the same.

Suddenly, Scott, the only one of thousands of drivers that happened to pass by, suddenly went into his car took out his wallet and removed an identification card from it. He handed it to me and said "Romel, you know I worked at that Butler County Jail!" The very same jail Ian was remanded at. He went on to suggest that maybe if we go to the jail and he flashed his I.D., explained everything to the prison officers that maybe they would allow us to talk to Ian. If he had gotten arrested with his apartment keys in his pocket, there was the possibility that they could even release them to us.

It sounded like a brilliant plan to my ears. I knew that this was what God had in store when Scott came back for me on I275, why he offered to take me all the way to my final destination and why God did not allow the directions to show up on his GPS when we first looked it up. I could only imagine Scott dropping me off at Victory Drive without us knowing Ian was in jail, I would have still been standing outside there waiting for Ian to come home.

We made our way to the Butler County Jail and Scott was able to speak to the persons working there. Within fifteen minutes I had the keys to Ian's apartment in my hands. "What's that address again?" Scott asked with a boastfulness that could only come from the spirit of the power of God working in him. "8 West Victory Drive, Hamilton, Ohio. 45013" I blurted out whilst pounding my legs with my fist in utter excitement about the great and marvelous thing God had just done in my own presence. Once again I was reassured in my heart that I was stepping in the right direction. It was not astonishing to us when the GPS found the address this third time around as Scott typed it in; reaffirming that it was the doing of the Most High.

Scott's wife called him and he had to hurry home so he dropped me off back at Ian's mother's house and Ronny took me over to the apartment, but not before I ate some steak that he had just finished grilling. Thank God for Scott Rimer! He literally saved my life, like an angel sent by God. After being totally worn out from everything that happened over the course of that day, things were finally looking up.

Chapter XXIII

The RRIM Mission

I turned the key and pushed the door to Ian's apartment as hard as I could, it was jammed. Ronny and Patti warned me that the place was in a mess and that all the clothes and household items were randomly scattered around. It appeared as though bandits and robbers had ransacked and looted everything. However I was still not prepared for the amount of work that had to be done in order to restore the place to a livable state. I threw out eleven large bags of trash, cleaned the floor, the bathroom, the kitchen and got rid of the awful smell that was resonating throughout the whole place. Finally I was able to bed down, and bed down I did! When all the work was finished I slept like a baby for fourteen hours.

After resting, I decided that I had to come up with a plan to get Ian out of jail. I didn't feel comfortable staying in an apartment that I had no clue about, this was America! I didn't fully understand how the rent and all the utilities were being paid, but most of all, I wanted someone around me when I started to do what is was that I had in my heart intended to do.

My laptop with my manuscript on its hard drive was seemingly lost to me, being twelve hours away in a pawn shop in Brooklyn. However I knew exactly what I had to do, but I was scared to do it. I made all sorts of excuses before the Lord, telling Him of how untrained and ill equipped I was, and without resources. I got on the phone and convinced Jameel to leave Buffalo and to come at once to meet me in Ohio, "the place we should have gone to in the first place" I told him. It was easy to convince him to take the eight hour bus ride across a few states because things were not going too well for him in New York. America had proven to be a bit harder than he had expected, different from what millions of others across the world dream it to be.

When he got to Cincinnati I met him as he got off the Megabus and we took one of the city buses to Tri-County mall, the closest stop to Hamilton. Ronny picked us up and took us to the family house where all had gathered, waiting to meet my Jameel. The Marcum/Page family had a long relationship with people from Trinidad and Tobago as they knew maybe a half dozen Trini's before meeting Jameel.

The following day I persuaded Jameel to sell his Samsung Galaxy Note II, a phone I bought for him April 21st when we first arrived. He sold it and we got $150.00 for the $700.00 phone. We took that money and bought twenty white t-shirts and printed on them "RRIM" on the front of each of them that Friday afternoon. The following day we walked along Main Street from the mile and a half stretch on the West Side of Hamilton where the apartment was, to the North End where the family lived. We encountered a street evangelist name Frank who was passing out 'Tracks' on the sidewalk. We stopped and talked with him for a few minutes before trading phone numbers and addresses, after which Frank offered to give Jameel and I a lift to our Greenwood Avenue destination. Later that afternoon, we invited Frank back to the apartment where we held a prayer and worship session, just the three of us, connected by God's Holy Spirit.

I could honestly say that Ian's apartment was by far the best place of abode I ever had in my life up to that point. In American standards it was nothing but the bare basics, a one bedroom with a small kitchen and living room. The bathroom was so tiny that whenever I would sit down on the toilet seat, my knees would jam against the heater that was jammed to both the wall and the tub. But at least there was a tub! At first the apartment with its nicely carpeted floor and standard window blinds was all mines, then when Jameel came we shared it. We had the best of times. We spent most of our waking hours reading the gospel accounts of Jesus Christ and the beyond amazing writings of the Apostle Paul, but it was the writings of Luke that we spent most of our first month reading over and over again the Acts of the Apostles.

It was evident to us and to those that we encountered in those early months that the presence of the Holy Spirit flowed from within our beings. No one was able to deny that God was with us. Jameel and I always saw that to be something everyone admitted to us and we declared it to ourselves privately many times; Emmanuel, God is with us!

In no time at all, we were able to come up with the $880.00 needed to bail Ian out of jail, all to the glory of our God who enabled us to rescue a friend in his time of need. Ian honestly was only guilty of being too drunk and hanging out with the wrong people. He had no idea that he was at the site of a crime when the police awoke him and he couldn't have taken the stolen items back to his own apartment then returned to pass out on the front lawn of the crime scene. However the main reason I just had to bail him out was mostly my own guilt over the whole thing, things that I have no control over always seem to take a hold of me. I felt guilty for Ian being in jail, my reason being that if I had gone to Cincinnati earlier in April, as was my plan instead of going to Buffalo, that maybe, just maybe I might have been able to convince Ian not to hang with such a crowd, and maybe about controlling his alcohol intake.

However, we all know that God is always working something out by using our lives, though things that may seem plain and ordinary, simple and even boring and sometimes meaningless, God is actually working on His master plan of His origin in order to put together the grand picture, His purpose for your life. Ian got out of jail and recommitted his life to the Lord. He stopped hanging out with most of the people that he had esteemed to be his friends.

I myself stayed in Hamilton from August 2013 until February 2014. I shared my life story testimony with around fifty congregations during that time period. The first of which was Grace United Methodist Church, located just opposite Victory Drive. It was a church that became very near and dear to my heart. It was the third Sunday in the hot summer month of August. Jameel and I walked boldly and confidently into the sanctuary of Grace United Methodist, both sporting the RRIM t-shirts we made the Friday before.

Pastor Andrew, the then assistant pastor at the church stopped pulling strings on the guitar he was practicing on in between his Sunday morning services. He smiled as he looked at us walking up the church's center aisle, coming towards him at the altar uniformed in a distinctively marked t-shirt, a marking he had not recalled seeing before. The senior pastor, J.C. Collins was away on a medical trip, having surgery done on a knee that gave him some trouble ever since his service in the U.S. Army. Andrew was left with the responsibilities of conducting the church's affairs and preaching the Sunday morning sermons while J.C. was gone. It was a task he knew he could accomplish, not just by his own effort but by solely trusting in Christ to direct his every step.

"What does RRIM stand for?" He asked us with a big smile, neatly combed brown hair and bright green eyes as we neared the altar. "Romel Ravello's International Ministries" I replied aloud. "Awesome! Are you guys going to join us for the service?" he asked. "Yes indeed" I quipped "I hope to share my testimony with you guys this morning" I informed him. It shocked me when he replied "that's awesome" as he walked down the aisle and met us with a hand shake and a warm hug as he introduced himself. He embraced us as brothers, like true brothers, it was kind of strange to me. Even though I had experienced the feeling of the brotherly love of Christ in Buffalo, I really was not expecting to find it in this small Ohio town where so many people had already yelled many racial remarks to us as they drove past us walking along the Main/High Street.

"We'll let you share your testimony first, then I'll preach" Andrew immediately informed me. "Wow! Okay" I blurted out. I was utterly surprised; this guy didn't know a single thing about me. He had never heard a word of my testimony. He had never before seen me in his life, had not heard of my name or my story from anyone, but he had already, by trusting Christ alone, allotted me a five minute time slot on that morning's schedule. I told him that we would go next door and have breakfast before the service started and be right back, but Jameel at once realized that I was trying to take a minute to go before the Lord in prayer secretly. "It got to be soul food you talking about, because we ain't got no money to buy nothing to eat over there!" he chuckled at me as we walked back out the front door ."But you know that!" I replied with a big grin on my face. We were broke, but we were happy and content knowing that we were where God wanted us to be, where He could be able to use my life story to touch someone's heart. We asked God for His guidance, wisdom and for His power to flow through my words. We prayed that God would let His words come from my mouth and not the words of my own meditation.

We went back into the chapel after having a belly full of spiritual bread and before the service began I had the opportunity to give pastor Andrew a little bit of insight as to the aspects of my life which I was about to share with the congregation that he was entrusted with. When he heard my story, he thanked God that he gave me the opportunity and he became excited for the church to hear what I had to say. They would turn out to be congregation number one of a ten thousand congregation mission.

I shared about five to seven minutes of my life story testimony to the church's congregation of about sixty people that morning. The crowd comprised mainly of senior citizens, most of them being women. Many had tears that flowed as they all stood on their feet applauding my struggles while they unanimously thank God for the love, mercy and grace He poured out on my life thus far. It was all so amazing the response I got! Everyone stood as they applauded and thanked God because of me, people were racing to the front of the altar to hug me, shaking my hands and patting me on the shoulder.

I could have never imagined people being so overjoyed to hear about my hardships. But it was not the hardships of a small child that brought delight to their hearts, it was the power of God's saving grace, and that was certainly something to rejoice about! Pastor Andrew was all the more happy for allowing this stranger to have a microphone given him that morning to share what they expressed to be one of the most powerful testimonies they ever heard.

Victory Heights Pentecostal was up next, where I spoke for about twenty minutes. Jameel dubbed the pastor as "The Fire Man" as he spoke with such passion and energy after I spoke. We had a great time there but the mission always called us to move forward. That Wednesday night we visited Fire House Church and I spoke there as well. The next Sunday we visited the "Christ Tabernacle Apostolic Church" and there I was for the first time "on fire". We visited a couple more churches; some I spoke at, some turned us down. Nevertheless, all in all we were having a great time experiencing the power and the mercies of the God that we were now for the first time so eager to serve, the Lord Jesus Christ.

I spoke in Hamilton, Oxford and Brookville, Indiana all thanks to the help of Tim, an ordained minister of church. It was not too far from the Immanuel Baptist Church which is located at 1770 Eaton Rd. Hamilton, Ohio. The big white church at the top of the hill in the west side of Hamilton, the one overlooking Hamilton High School. The following Sunday, I spoke at both the 8:00am and the 10:30am services at Park Avenue United Methodist Church. After speaking at Park Avenue United Methodist Church one Sunday morning, a lot of people came up and hugged me and shook my hand, some… a lot, of them stuck money in my hands and pockets. There was this little old lady that came up and kissed me on both cheeks and slipped me her business card. She was Miss Karen Cocina, the owner of Main Street School House Inc. At the back of the card she wrote "Two bedroom and bath upstairs apartment available to you". All she said to me was that we were welcome to come at anytime.

This opportunity had served us well as it was now the three of us sharing Ian's one bedroom apartment. Jameel and I moved to 116 North 7th Street into Ms. Karen's house leaving John (who is John, where/when did he come?) in the apartment to take care of it and himself. After a couple months I returned to stay with John, just around the thanksgiving holidays and then into the Christmas season.

Sometime during that period while speaking in many different churches in the community, I spoke at a very small neat community church called Headwaters Contemporary Christian Community. It was pastored by a very friendly round bellied guy named Earnie, my thoughts were that he would make a perfect Santa Claus! It was here that I met the members of the Landon family. I spoke at a great deal of churches and community groups in the greater Cincinnati area, far too many to list and was past forty by the time New Years Day arrived. On New Years Day 2014, David Landon took me to a house party that one of his friend's sister was having at her home. I was told that a lot of believers from several different churches were going be there and I would share my testimony with them in the hopes of creating opportunities to share at other churches. Linda and Roy were amazing hosts on that cold Ohio holiday. Their house was beautiful, warm and inviting. It had been the biggest house I had ever step foot in up to that point. There at that house, was where I met Al and Nancy Sabatka and it didn't take long at all for the Sabatka's to invite me to come spend some time at their house.

Chapter XXIV

The Adventures of Romel and John

By mid-January, John and I were California dreaming, thinking about the warm sun, the cool breeze and the beautiful beaches that were sweeping the west coast. The bitter cold in Cincinnati was becoming more than we were willing to put up with. School was closed, offices shut down and the state department was advising everyone to remain indoors and in warm conditions. The temperature and wind-chill reached record breaking levels. It was so cold that whenever I stepped outside with my dog Diamond, it felt like my body was so cold that it was on fire.

Somehow I was able to convince John to quit his job, leave everything and come along with me as I chased after the glory of the Lord Jesus Christ. Our first step was to spend three weeks at the home of Al and Nancy Sabatka in Milford, Ohio as they boasted of having a really nice two bedroom basement apartment that was freely and readily available for me and my companions. I felt that staying with them would dramatically reduce our expenditure bill and help us to save as much money as possible for our big move to the golden coast.

I can honestly say that my mission in Los Angles really started there, at the Sabatka home. They attended the Christian Life Center CLC Church, the same one as Roy and Linda and many others that were at the New Year's Eve party at their house. I was given the opportunity by Pastor Lonnie to share my testimony there with the entire congregation and after ten minutes, Pastor Lonnie kept urging me to keep sharing and not to stop. I ended up speaking for about thirty five minutes.

The members of CLC Church blessed me with a Love Offering totaling about $2,800.00. The Sabatka's were blown away by the generosity shown to me by their very own home church. Al spoke about the money all night and all day the next day. He spoke about it so much that when we returned to CLC Church the following night I called Pastor Lonnie into his office and donated the total sum I received to two of the church's missionaries in Asia, Karen-Beth and Jeffery. Al was extremely upset at my decision and sought to convince me that I need that money for John and I to get to Los Angeles. He was so outspoken about it that he even convinced John that I was clearly in the wrong for doing what I did, especially since our days staying at his house were numbered.

John was furious when he heard what I did. He didn't as yet understand how to trust that if God was able to do it once, He could do it again and again. "No Romel, I can't do this!" John said to me as he headed to the basement "this is crazy. That was the most amount of cash I've ever seen in my life and you just gave it away. I'm going back home" he continued as he went into his room and started to pack his bags. I decided to give him a minute and went to my own room. I knew that God would make another way and shut the mouth of my skeptics.

I got on my laptop and started to search Facebook for new friends. I changed my location to Los Angeles, California and in the search bar I wrote "Follower of Jesus Christ". I sent a friend request to the top three names that showed up in the search results, the first of which was Jesse Reyes, then Marshall Tubbs and one other. I was able to soon after convince my traveling companion to trust that I knew what I was doing, I assured him that in less than one week we were going to be driving our own car to California and that God would bless us with even more money for our trip because of our faithfulness.

Less than a week later, John and I were driving down Interstate 75 in our very own two door Acura sports car on our way to L.A.! God had come through for us. Not only did we have more than enough money to get there, John had also just received his tax returns and Robert and Ann Brown had committed to purchasing 500 copies of my book (when did you finish writing the book, and got it published?) for us to sell while on our trip. To subsidize our income, they gave us one hundred copies up front and pledged another four hundred when we settled there and had an address for them to be posted to. Jesse Reyes had also already accepted my friend request and told me about his church Reality L.A. Jameel stayed in Cincinnati.

It took us 46 hours to drive nonstop from Cincinnati to Manhattan Beach in Los Angeles. We had determined within ourselves to not stop until we "reached the ocean". I had no driver's license, I lost my passport, no ID card or any form of identification, but it was impossible for John to have driven all the way there. I drove some 17 hours and he drove the rest. I think the best part of the road trip was when we both started to realize how big the sky really was when we saw it as we rolled through the plains of Oklahoma, New Mexico, Arizona and Texas.

When we did get to the ocean, our spirits were once again rejuvenated. We had a few dollars so we roamed about looking for a hotel to check into in the middle of downtown Los Angeles. It didn't take us long to find Reality LA Church smack in the center of Hollywood. I began selling the books that I had remaining. After being there for about an hour, two guys walked around the corner and looked at us smiling "I know you guys! You're John and your Romel" one of them said to us. He was Jesse Reyes, the first follower of Christ I found on Facebook in the Los Angeles area, the one I had sent the friend request to!

For John and I California was great. We had some good times and we had times where we were both sleeping in our car, rationing one Lil Caesar's pizza and a 2 liter soda a day! But the awesome thing was that the Lord was with us in every step we took! He was there and He made a way where there was no way. In spite of the blessings, or rather along with the blessings, a lot was required. Sometimes even I felt like it was going to be too much for me to bear. The only thing that kept me going was the fact that I knew what God was doing, I knew that He was working everything out. John however had not gotten to that point yet. It became a bit too much for him and he felt like it was time for him to go home. There was no way I could have blamed him we spent many months together and John accompanied me to more than forty more churches along my mission before he jumped on a bus and headed back home and so our adventures together ended.

Chapter XXV

That California Life

Jesse Reyes and Bryan Bergman are some of the best and closet brothers I've ever been blessed with in my life. Coming from the frozen over state of Ohio, it felt good to wear t-shirts and shorts once again. It felt even better to have friends and peers to relate to, hang out with, pray, read the bible and go to church with. They introduced me to Tanya Chisholm, Will Barker, Kirk Friggins, Bree Bond, Tommy Snider and many, many other Hollywood personalities with whom they were friends with.

I stayed with Cartoon Network's producer, Tommy Snider at his North Hollywood condominium. I also spent a few days with the lone female star of Nickelodeon's Big Time Rush and spoke at a number of difference places all across Hollywood. I made money by selling copies of my book outside of Brooke Brothers clothing store on the corner of Santa Monica Boulevard and Rodeo Drive in Beverly Hills and started renting a suite at a Motel6 in Van Nuys.

Not long after Jameel came to meet me from Cincinnati and he too had the opportunity to experience the California life that most people could only dream about. We woke up, visited Jesse and Bryan, sold books, ate lunch, found a church or community group to speak at, and then headed to Venice beach. That was our routine every day. From Los Angeles we headed to San Francisco to pay a visit to Aaron, one of Jameel's childhood friends in a small wine town called Napa. From there it was back to Hollywood and as soon as we arrived, my car broke down.

It cost $1700.00 to repair the car because the gearbox was destroyed due to my lack of experience driving a manual car leading to a burnt out clutch. Kirk Friggins graciously paid for the repairs in full. By this time I had spoken to 130 congregations and it was time for Jameel and I to start to making our way from California across to Chicago.

We drove from Los Angeles to Las Vegas where we stopped at the Caesars Palace for a few brief moments. Jameel wanted us to stay there for a few days and sell some books, but I couldn't bring myself to sell a book all about what the Lord had done in my life in the center of Sin City. I convinced him that we should move on.

From there we headed up into Utah and then across to Colorado by way of the Rocky Mountains. While up in the Rockies, there was a snow storm that got so severe, I was forced to pull off the road and park the car in the parking lot of a gas station to wait for better driving conditions. I remember saying to Jameel "Bro, I'm not trying to play a superhero role here tonight, I can't even see in from of me so I'm pulling over", that was shortly after 11:00p.m. Finally at about 5:30a.m., we were back on the road again. Our mountain trip was all downhill from there. We survived the Rockies and were now heading into the plain open fields of Colorado.

I drove straight past Denver in a bid to make up for lost time when all of a sudden the engine of the car went dead and I was forced to pull over again, eight hundred miles short of Chicago. I parked the car on the shoulder of the Interstate and with the biggest smile on my face I got out, threw my hands up in the air and began thanking and praising God for His faithfulness, His love and His grace over our lives.

At first Jameel didn't quite understand what I was so jubilant about. I had to take a minute and remind him of the deadly snowstorm we just came through and how amazing it was that God allowed us to reach down into the hot dry desert before the car broke down. Then his eyes were opened and the praises started flowing from his mouth as well. Then there was His voice

"Do you trust me Romel?"

"Of course Lord" was my reply. Then the Lord said,

"Okay if you guys push the car just 200 meters down the road there, you will find the help you need. There's a house there and they will help you."

When I told this to Jameel he started to get angry and maybe rightfully so. We were in the middle of the desert, in the flat open plains. Our eyes could see a hundred miles in every direction. "Romel, why should we push the car? There is nothing there, 200 meters is only a stone's throw away and there's nothing in sight. It would be crazy for us to waste our energy pushing the car." I told Him that God had never been wrong before and if He said the house was there, then it would be there. "We walk by faith remember" was all I said to him but he was not hearing it. He got even more upset, but my faith was unmoved.

I reminded him of all the many times when God told me something and it came to pass just as the Lord said it would. By this time I had over ten points of reference which I could draw from about God speaking and His words coming to pass in our lives. Maybe the heat was getting to Jameel and he was not thinking clear for a short period of time because when he finally agreed for us to push the car, he insisted on him pushing it by himself. "No! You don't push, I'll push, the Lord spoke to you and told you it have a house right there, like you're some kinda prophet or something, so you don't push. But Romel, when we get there, God really better be with you!"

My heart raced all the more as the car started to roll. My friend was so upset with me because he couldn't see, but neither could I! I had to trust and believe God. One hundred meters and nothing, one hundred and fifty meters and I still couldn't see any house. I was so scared of losing my friendship out here that I started to command the house into existence. One hundred and seventy five meters and still nothing. Then, as the car rolled a few more inches suddenly the Lord opened both of our eyes! I jumped out the car rejoicing! Jameel started yelling "Romel you're a prophet! Romel you're a prophet!"

The whole time we were thinking that the desert was this flat open place, but when the Lord opened our eyes we realized that there was something like humps and valleys and hills in the seemingly flat desert and right there, fifteen meters ahead of us was a drop or slope and on that slope was a house whose roof we finally got a glimpse of. We rejoiced and praised God like it was the first time He had ever done something spectacular for us, but the fact of the matter was seeing God's glory was becoming common practice for us. We were just ten miles from Julesburg, Colorado.

It was in Julesburg that I finally became convinced about what I wanted to do with my life. Most people sit around waiting on life to happen, many brilliant minds wasted waiting on an opportunity to come their way, it never did. They stay content with the level of life they were born into and rarely ever attempt to do anything to change it. Not me! Not Romel Ravello! Not anymore. I no longer had to ask the question "What are you going to do with your life?" My life's journey was now really about to begin. My life had never been what you could call ordinary, nor could it have been described simply. It was in fact, 'a roller coaster' but I was now certain that the Living God was with me.

I want to be just like Paul! That my life forever will bring glory to His Holy name for He is worthy beyond measure of all praises and of all glory and all honor forever and ever Amen, and the journey of my life along that path had now fully begun. Hallelujah!

TO BE CONTINUED...

Excerpts from the Scriptures taken from *AMG International NIV, 1996,* by International Bible Society.

Front Photography credit: Kimlee Bunraj

Made in the USA
Columbia, SC
11 May 2017